Gooseberry Patch®

Ready, Set,
EAT!

Gooseberry Patch
2545 Farmers Dr., #380
Columbus, OH 43235

www.gooseberrypatch.com

1•800•854•6673

Copyright 2007, Gooseberry Patch 978-1-62093-136-3
Fifth Printing, December, 2013

Do you have a tried & true recipe...

tip, craft or memory that you'd like to see featured in a **Gooseberry Patch** book? Visit our website at **www.gooseberrypatch.com**, register and follow the easy steps to submit your favorite family recipe. Or send them to us at:

*Gooseberry Patch
2545 Farmers Dr., #380
Columbus, OH 43235*

Don't forget to include the number of servings your recipe makes, plus your name, address, phone number and e-mail address. If we select your recipe, your name will appear right along with it... and you'll receive a **FREE** copy of the book!

Contents

Dedication

To busy families everywhere
that want to enjoy
dinnertime...together!

Appreciation

A hearty thanks to all
of you who shared your favorite recipes
for getting dinner on the table...fast!

BEAT the CLOCK

Meals in
30 minutes

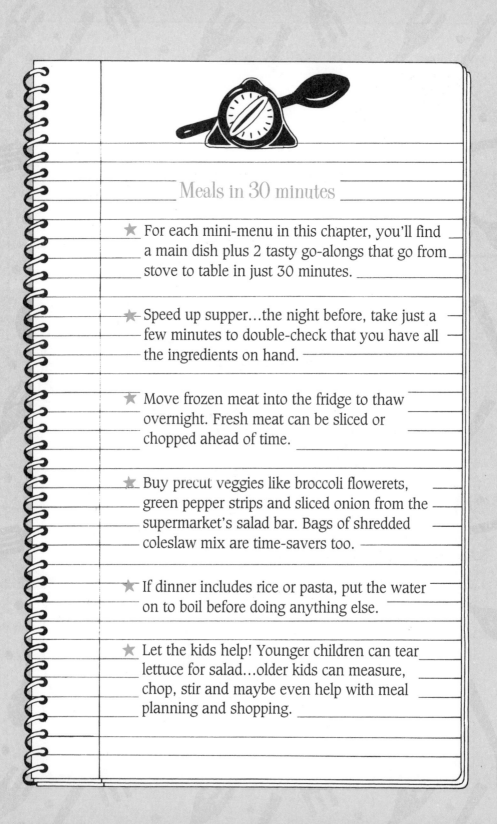

Meals in 30 minutes

★ For each mini-menu in this chapter, you'll find a main dish plus 2 tasty go-alongs that go from stove to table in just 30 minutes.

★ Speed up supper...the night before, take just a few minutes to double-check that you have all the ingredients on hand.

★ Move frozen meat into the fridge to thaw overnight. Fresh meat can be sliced or chopped ahead of time.

★ Buy precut veggies like broccoli flowerets, green pepper strips and sliced onion from the supermarket's salad bar. Bags of shredded coleslaw mix are time-savers too.

★ If dinner includes rice or pasta, put the water on to boil before doing anything else.

★ Let the kids help! Younger children can tear lettuce for salad...older kids can measure, chop, stir and maybe even help with meal planning and shopping.

Beat the Clock

Pork & Apple Skillet Supper

Carol Lytle
Columbus, OH

A hearty, tummy-warming dinner...ready in just a few minutes.

2 T. butter
1/2 t. garlic, minced
1/2 t. salt
1/4 t. pepper

4 3 to 4-oz. pork cube steaks
1 onion, sliced
2 Granny Smith apples, cored
   and sliced

Melt butter in a skillet until sizzling; stir in seasonings. Add pork steaks and onion. Cook over medium-high heat, turning occasionally, until pork is browned, 4 to 6 minutes. Add apples; continue cooking, stirring occasionally, just until tender, 2 to 3 minutes. Place pork steaks on plates; top with apples and onion. Serves 4.

Cabbage & Caraway Sauté:
Melt 2 tablespoons butter in a large skillet over medium heat. Add one 16-ounce package shredded cabbage; sauté until crisp-tender. Remove from heat; stir in one teaspoon caraway seeds. Serves 4.

Sweet Potato Wedges:
Peel 2 sweet potatoes and slice into wedges; toss with olive oil. Bake at 375 degrees until fork-tender, about 20 to 25 minutes. Drizzle with honey, if desired. Serves 4.

You've put dinner on the table in just 30 minutes... congratulations! Now relax and enjoy a pleasant family meal...hold the phone, please!

Instant Chicken Parmesan

Megan Naumovski
Delaware, OH

This is quick & easy...it's a favorite meal in our home.

28-oz. jar spaghetti sauce
4 to 6 frozen breaded chicken
  patties

4 to 6 slices provolone cheese
1 to 2 T. grated Parmesan
  cheese

Spread sauce in an ungreased 13"x9" baking pan; arrange frozen chicken patties on top. Place a slice of provolone on top of each patty; sprinkle with Parmesan cheese. Bake, covered, at 350 degrees for 20 minutes. Uncover and bake for an additional 5 to 10 minutes, or until cheese is bubbly. Serves 4 to 6.

Garlic Vermicelli Toss:
Toss 4 cups hot cooked vermicelli or angel hair pasta with 2 tablespoons olive oil, 2 teaspoons minced garlic and one cup grated Parmesan cheese. Add salt and pepper to taste. Serves 4.

Italian Green Beans:
Toss 2 cups cooked green beans with Italian salad dressing; sprinkle with grated Parmesan cheese, if desired. Serves 4.

Set a regular theme for each night of the week... Italian Night, Soup & Salad Night, Mexican Night or Casserole Night, based on your family's favorites. Meal planning is a snap!

Holly's Creamy Garlic Chicken

Holly Sutton
Grahamsville, NY

Flatten the chicken between 2 pieces of wax paper...it will cook up quickly and evenly.

2 t. oil
4 boneless, skinless chicken
   breasts
1/4 c. mayonnaise-type
   salad dressing

2 c. frozen stir-fry vegetables
1 T. soy sauce
2 cloves garlic, minced
3 c. cooked rice

Heat oil in a large skillet over medium heat. Add chicken; cook for 6 minutes, turning once. Stir in remaining ingredients except rice. Cover and cook 7 minutes, or until chicken is cooked through. Serve over hot rice. Serves 4.

Toasty Garlic Bread:
Combine 1/2 cup softened butter, one clove minced garlic and one tablespoon chopped fresh parsley. Spread on a loaf of French bread, split lengthwise. Broil for one to 2 minutes, until lightly golden. Makes one loaf.

Lemon Sorbet:
Scoop one pint of lemon sorbet into individual serving dishes. Top each with 2 tablespoons raspberries and 1/4 cup pineapple tidbits. Serves 4.

Speedy Sausage & Black-Eyed Peas

Narita Roady
Pryor, OK

*Pop a tray of cornbread muffins in the oven
to round out this meal.*

1 lb. ground pork sausage
1/2 c. onion, chopped
1 jalapeño pepper, seeded
   and chopped

16-oz. can black-eyed peas,
   drained and rinsed

Brown sausage, onion and jalapeño in a skillet over medium heat until sausage is done; drain. Stir in peas and heat through. Serves 4.

Spinach-Tomato Sauté:

Sauté a 16-ounce package of fresh spinach in one tablespoon olive oil over medium heat until wilted. Sprinkle with salt and pepper to taste; remove to serving platter. Add 2 cloves minced garlic to skillet; cook for one minute. Add one chopped tomato and heat through. Spoon mixture over spinach; drizzle with one tablespoon balsamic vinegar. Serves 4.

Cinnamon-Sugar Apples:

Combine 1/4 cup sugar and 2 teaspoons cinnamon; set aside. Core, peel and slice 2 to 3 apples into wedges; sprinkle with cinnamon-sugar. Microwave in a microwave-safe dish on high setting until tender. Serves 4.

Beat the Clock

Sweet-and-Sour Hot Dogs

Barbara Stienstra
Goshen, NY

I like to spoon this over a bed of salad greens...a pretty presentation for dinner guests.

6-oz. can unsweetened
   pineapple juice
3/4 c. cider vinegar
3/4 c. catsup
1/3 c. soy sauce
1 T. cornstarch
16-oz. pkg. hot dogs, sliced
8-oz. can pineapple chunks,
   drained

8-oz. can sliced water
   chestnuts, drained
8-oz. can bamboo shoots,
   drained
4-1/2 oz. can sliced
   mushrooms, drained
1 c. green or red pepper, cubed
1/4 c. green onion, sliced

Mix together first 5 ingredients in a medium saucepan; cook over medium heat, stirring frequently, until mixture comes to a boil and sauce is clear. Combine remaining ingredients in a large microwave-safe bowl; pour sauce over top. Microwave on high setting for 5 minutes, until heated through. Serves 4.

Pimento Rice:
Prepare 4 servings instant rice according to package directions. Stir in one 2-ounce jar of chopped pimentos. Sprinkle with salt and pepper to taste. Serves 4.

Peanut Butter Ice Cream Delight:
Soften one pint vanilla ice cream; swirl in peanut butter to taste. Scoop into bowls; top with chocolate sandwich cookie crumbs. Serves 4.

Make a game of table talk! Write fun questions on file cards...
what kind of animal would you like to be?
what's your favorite book? and so on. Pull a different
card each night to talk about.

Pepper-Crusted Salmon

Stacie Mickley
Gooseberry Patch

You'll want to use freshly ground pepper to get the crust crispy.

1/4 c. soy sauce
2 cloves garlic, pressed
4 t. lemon juice
2 t. sugar

4 6-oz. salmon fillets
1 T. pepper
1/4 c. olive oil

Combine first 4 ingredients in a plastic zipping bag; add salmon. Refrigerate for 10 minutes. Remove salmon from bag; discard marinade. Pat dry; press pepper into both sides of salmon. Heat oil in a large heavy skillet over medium heat; sauté salmon 2 to 3 minutes per side, or until it flakes easily. Drain on paper towels. Serves 4.

Shiitake Rice:

Prepare 2 cups instant rice according to package directions, using chicken broth instead of water. Add one 4-ounce can shiitake mushrooms; garnish with 1/4 cup chopped green onion. Serves 4.

Sesame Broccoli Sauté:

Heat one tablespoon sesame oil over medium heat; add 2 cups chopped broccoli and one tablespoon sesame seed. Sauté for 2 minutes; add one sliced green pepper and cook until crisp-tender. Serves 4.

Welcome

Real cloth napkins make mealtime just a little more special. Stitch fun charms to napkin rings, so everyone can identify their own napkin easily.

Beat the Clock

Chili-Rubbed Steaks

Beverly Ray
Brandon, FL

Rubs are a great quick way to give steaks delicious flavor.

1 T. ground cumin
2 t. chili powder
1/2 t. salt

1/8 t. pepper
3 boneless sirloin steaks,
    about 1/2-inch thick

Mix together seasonings and rub on both sides of steaks; let stand for 5 to 10 minutes. Lightly oil grill rack. Grill steaks over medium heat for 3 to 5 minutes per side for medium-rare. Slice each steak in half; mound each with a generous portion of Chunky Guacamole Salsa. Serve any remaining guacamole on the side. Serves 6.

Chunky Guacamole Salsa:
Place 2 peeled and diced avocados in a medium bowl. Add 2 chopped plum tomatoes and one chopped jalapeño pepper; set aside. Mix together 2 tablespoons each lime juice, chopped shallots and chopped fresh cilantro. Add 1-1/2 teaspoons ground cumin and 1/2 teaspoon salt in a small bowl; whisk in 2 tablespoons oil. Pour over avocado mixture; mix well. Serves 6.

Chocolate-Caramel Pudding:
Prepare one large package chocolate pudding mix according to package directions. Spoon into 6 serving glasses. Top each with 2 ladyfingers; drizzle with caramel ice cream topping. Serves 6.

Chicken Alfredo Pizza

Christa Kerr
DuBois, PA

For an even speedier pizza, use a ready-to-bake crust.

3 6-1/2 oz. pkgs. pizza
   crust mix
1 lb. boneless, skinless
   chicken breasts
1 t. Italian seasoning
1 T. oil

16-oz. jar Alfredo sauce
8-oz. pkg. shredded Italian-
   blend cheese
12-oz. pkg. sliced mushrooms
1 onion, sliced and separated
   into rings

Prepare pizza crust according to package directions; divide dough
evenly between two lightly greased 12" pizza pans. Press dough
into pans; set aside. Sprinkle chicken with Italian seasoning; sauté
in oil until cooked through. Cool; cut into 1/2-inch slices. Set
aside. Spread half of the sauce on each crust; top with half each of
chicken, cheese, mushrooms and onion. Bake at 450 degrees for
15 to 20 minutes; cut into wedges. Serves 6 to 8.

Mamma Mia Salad:

Toss together one package salad greens, one chopped tomato,
1/2 chopped cucumber and a 4-ounce package of crumbled feta
cheese. Add Italian salad dressing to taste; sprinkle with grated
Parmesan cheese, if desired. Serves 6.

Berry Good Dessert:

In a large bowl, stir together one 32-ounce container vanilla
yogurt, one cup granola, one cup raspberries and one sliced
banana. Serves 6.

Beefy Filled Hard Rolls

Diann Stewart
Las Vegas, NV

*Growing up in Southern California, we went to the beach a lot.
These rolls were one of our favorite things to bring.*

2 lbs. ground beef
1/4 c. onion, diced
10-3/4 oz. can cream of
   mushroom soup

1/2 c. Colby cheese, grated
salt and pepper to taste
12 small French hard rolls,
   sliced and hollowed out

Brown ground beef with onion in a skillet over medium heat;
drain. Add soup and simmer for 5 minutes. Stir in cheese, salt and
pepper; cook until cheese melts. Fill rolls with meat mixture and
top with top halves of rolls. Serves 6.

Corn Salad:

Combine two 15-1/4 ounce cans drained corn, one 16-ounce can
drained and rinsed black beans, one chopped tomato, 3 chopped
green onions and one tablespoon ground cumin. Drizzle with lime
juice to taste; chill or serve at room temperature. Serves 6.

Melon Patch Sherbet:

Cut one large sweet, ripe cantaloupe into 6 wedges.
Top each wedge with a scoop of favorite sherbet. Serves 6.

Mmm...mashed potatoes are the ultimate comfort food.
Simmer potatoes in chicken broth instead
of water for delicious flavor.

Irene's Awesome Pork Tenderloins

Irene Robinson
Cincinnati, OH

A very flavorful meal for a family or dinner party.
Guests always ask me for this recipe.

1 t. seasoned salt
1/2 t. pepper
2 cloves garlic, minced

2 1-lb. pork tenderloins
6 slices bacon

Mix together salt, pepper and garlic; rub mix into tenderloins. Wrap each with bacon slices; secure with toothpicks. Grill over hot coals for 18 minutes, turning several times. Serves 6.

Honeyed Carrots:

Cook 3 cups of sliced carrots in a saucepan with water until tender; drain. Add one to 2 tablespoons honey and 2 teaspoons fresh chopped tarragon. Serves 6.

Snappy Apricot Ice Cream:

Scoop vanilla ice cream into 6 serving dishes; top each with 1/4 cup warmed apricot preserves and sprinkle with gingersnap crumbs. Serves 6.

The aroma of bread baking is so comforting...even refrigerated rolls will make your kitchen smell like baking bread. Dress up rolls with a drizzle of melted butter and a dash of dried oregano before baking...almost as good as homemade.

Beat the Clock

Chicken & Artichoke Pasta

Linda Behling
Cecil, PA

This is one of our favorites...it's a great way to use leftovers.

4 cloves garlic, minced
1/4 c. olive oil
1 c. asparagus, sliced
4 c. bowtie pasta, cooked
1 bunch fresh basil, chopped
1 c. sun-dried tomatoes in oil

1 c. deli roast chicken, chopped
1 c. canned artichokes,
   chopped
salt and pepper to taste
Garnish: shredded Parmesan
   cheese

Sauté garlic in oil in a large pan over medium heat. Add asparagus; cook until crisp-tender. Fold in remaining ingredients except salt, pepper and cheese; mix well and heat through. Sprinkle with salt and pepper; garnish with cheese. Serves 4.

Zucchini Toss:

Sauté 3 to 4 sliced zucchini in one tablespoon oil until almost tender. Add one clove minced garlic; cook for one minute. Remove from heat; stir in one chopped tomato and one tablespoon chopped fresh basil. Serves 4.

Lemon-Blueberry Parfaits:

Combine 2 cups lemon yogurt and 1/2 cup blueberries. Spoon into individual serving dishes; top with dollops of whipped topping. Serves 4.

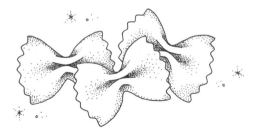

Zippy Broiled Catfish

Mardell Ross
Genoa, IL

Yummy! Garnish with lemon wedges and fresh parsley.

6 catfish fillets
1/4 c. lemon juice
1 t. salt

1/8 t. pepper
1 c. all-purpose flour
1-1/3 c. Italian salad dressing

Brush fillets with lemon juice; sprinkle with salt and pepper. Dredge fillets in flour. Arrange on a well-greased broiler pan; brush with salad dressing. Broil about 4 inches from heat source for 4 to 6 minutes, basting occasionally with salad dressing. Turn carefully; brush with additional salad dressing. Broil for 4 to 6 minutes, until fish flakes easily. Serves 6.

Cajun Cabbage:
Shred 1/2 head of cabbage; sauté in one tablespoon oil over medium heat. Add 1/2 teaspoon Cajun seasoning. Serves 4 to 6.

Cinnamon-Vanilla Pudding Parfaits:
Prepare one large package of instant vanilla pudding mix according to package directions; add cinnamon to taste. Layer pudding and whipped topping alternately in glass serving dishes; top with a cherry. Serves 4.

Lemony iced tea is so refreshing. Brew 9 teabags in 3 quarts boiling water for 5 minutes. Discard teabags. Stir in a 12-ounce can of frozen lemonade concentrate and a cup of sugar. Serve over ice...ahh!

Beat the Clock

Louisiana Shrimp Boil

Janet Bowlin
Fayetteville, AR

This is fun served outdoors on a picnic table...pass the paper towels!

2 onions, sliced
2 lemons, sliced
3-oz. pkg. crab boil seasoning
Optional: hot sauce to taste

16 new redskin potatoes
4 ears corn, husked and halved
2 lbs. uncooked medium
   shrimp in the shell

Fill a very large stockpot half full with water; add onions, lemons, seasoning and hot pepper sauce, if using. Bring water to a boil over medium-high heat; add potatoes and boil 10 minutes. Add corn; boil for 5 minutes. Add shrimp; boil until shrimp turn pink and float to the surface. Drain; serve on a large platter. Serves 4.

French Bread:
Bake one frozen loaf of French bread as directed on package; set aside. Blend together 1/2 cup softened butter, 2 cloves finely minced garlic and one tablespoon chopped fresh chives. Serve with sliced hot bread. Makes 4 to 6 servings.

Mint Chocolate Chip Pie:
Soften one quart mint chocolate chip ice cream. Spread into a graham cracker crust. Freeze until ready to serve. Serves 8 to 10.

Cover the picnic table with newspaper for a warm-weather meal...afterwards, just roll it up and toss away! Perfect for peel & eat shrimp, fried chicken and other tasty-but-messy suppers.

Savory Dijon-Style Chicken

Jen Danzeisen
Neshkoro, WI

The luscious sauce even makes frozen,
breaded chicken breasts taste scrumptious!

6 boneless, skinless chicken
   breasts
1 egg
1 c. all-purpose flour
1 t. pepper
1/4 to 1/2 c. butter-flavored
   shortening

1 t. Dijon mustard
1/3 c. dry white wine or
   chicken broth
1 T. honey
1/8 t. dill weed
3/4 c. whipping cream

Flatten chicken breasts to about 1/2-inch thick; set aside. Beat egg in a shallow bowl; mix flour and pepper in another shallow bowl. Dip chicken into egg; coat in flour mixture. Melt shortening in a skillet over medium heat. Cook chicken for about 6 minutes on each side, until golden and juices run clear. Remove from skillet; place in a lightly greased 13"x9" baking pan and keep warm. Stir together mustard, wine or broth, honey and dill weed in a saucepan over low heat until warmed. Gradually stir in cream; cook and stir until slightly thickened. Pour sauce over chicken; bake for 10 minutes at 350 degrees. Serves 4 to 6.

Speedy Linguine:
Cook an 8-ounce package of linguine pasta according to package directions. Drain; toss with 1/4 cup butter and sprinkle with one tablespoon poppy seed. Serves 4 to 6.

Root Beer Floats:
Scoop vanilla ice cream into 4 to 6 serving glasses; add root beer until glasses are almost full. Serve with straws and tall spoons. Serves 4 to 6.

Beat the Clock

Key West Citrus Chicken

Sandra Lee Smith
Arleta, CA

Delicious tropical flavors for a summer evening.

4 boneless, skinless chicken
  breasts
salt and pepper to taste
1/3 c. orange juice

3 cloves garlic, minced
1/4 t. ground ginger
1/8 t. red pepper flakes
Garnish: orange slices

Sprinkle chicken with salt and pepper; place in a skillet sprayed
with non-stick vegetable spray. Cook chicken over medium heat
until tender and no longer pink, 8 to 10 minutes, turning once.
Stir together orange juice, garlic, ginger and red pepper flakes in
a small bowl; pour into skillet. Bring to a boil; reduce heat and
simmer, uncovered, for 2 minutes. To serve, spoon pan juices
over chicken; top with orange slices. Serves 4.

Almond Rice:
Prepare 4 servings instant rice according to package directions;
stir in 1/2 cup toasted slivered almonds. Serves 4.

Broiled Pineapple Slices:
Sprinkle 8 pineapple slices with 1/4 cup brown sugar. Broil until
bubbly; sprinkle with cinnamon and top with scoops of vanilla ice
cream. Serves 4.

Fresh flowers are such a pick-me-up! Why not bring home
a casual bouquet from the supermarket to tuck into a
canning jar for a country-style arrangement in a jiffy.

Donna's Shrimp Scampi

Donna Eichner
Whitehall, PA

This recipe is always a hit with my family & friends.

1/2 c. butter
2 t. Worcestershire sauce
1/4 c. cooking sherry or
　chicken broth
1 to 2 t. garlic, minced
2 T. lemon juice
1 T. sugar

1 to 1-1/2 lbs. uncooked
　medium shrimp, cleaned
1/4 c. fresh parsley, minced
3 c. cooked rice
Garnish: grated Parmesan
　cheese

Melt butter in a saucepan over low heat. Stir in sauce, sherry or broth, garlic, lemon juice and sugar; mix well and remove from heat. Arrange shrimp in a single layer in a lightly greased 11"x7" baking pan. Spoon butter mixture over shrimp; sprinkle with parsley. Broil at medium heat for 5 minutes, until shrimp turn pink. Spoon over cooked rice; sprinkle with Parmesan cheese. Serves 4.

Roasted Asparagus:
Toss one pound asparagus with one tablespoon olive oil; arrange on a baking sheet. Sprinkle with salt to taste. Bake at 400 degrees for 8 to 10 minutes, until tender. Serves 4.

Creamy Peach Whirl:
In a blender, combine 2 cups peach slices, 2 cups vanilla ice cream, one cup milk and 2 tablespoons powdered sugar; process until smooth. Sprinkle with nutmeg. Serves 4.

Beat the Clock

Linguine in White Clam Sauce

Kathy Grashoff
Fort Wayne, IN

*Garnish with freshly shredded Parmesan cheese
for a special touch.*

2 T. olive oil
8 cloves garlic, chopped
1/2 c. fresh parsley, chopped
4 6-1/2 oz. cans chopped
   clams, drained and juice
   reserved
1/2 c. whipping cream
1 T. Worcestershire sauce

1/4 c. white wine or chicken
   broth
1 t. garlic salt
1 t. pepper
1 t. cayenne pepper
16-oz. pkg. linguine pasta,
   cooked

Heat oil in a skillet; add garlic and parsley. Sauté for 45 seconds;
stir in reserved clam juice, cream, Worcestershire sauce, wine
or broth and seasonings. Simmer for 10 minutes; mix in clams.
Simmer for 5 to 7 minutes; serve over hot cooked linguine.
Serves 6.

Citrus Broccoli:

Cut a head of broccoli into flowerets; steam until tender. Arrange
in a serving bowl; toss with 2 tablespoons butter, 1-1/2 teaspoons
orange zest, salt and pepper to taste. Serves 4 to 6.

Fruit Kabobs & Orange-Coconut Dip:

Make 10 kabobs with favorite fruits. Combine one 8-ounce
container vanilla yogurt, one tablespoon sweetened flaked coconut
and one tablespoon orange marmalade; stir well. Makes 10.

For a side dish that practically cooks itself, fill aluminum
foil packets with sliced fresh veggies. Top with seasoning
salt and 2 ice cubes, seal and bake at 450 degrees for
20 to 25 minutes. Delicious!

Chicken & Sausage Étouffée

Robin Dusenbery
San Antonio, TX

This recipe was passed down from my grandmother to my mom to me. Every time I make it, it brings me back to summer days in south Louisiana.

1 T. olive oil
1 onion, chopped
1 green pepper, chopped
2 stalks celery, chopped
1 lb. boneless, skinless chicken breast, cubed
1 lb. smoked sausage, sliced

2 10-oz. can tomatoes with chiles
6-oz. can tomato paste
2 10-3/4 oz. cans cream of mushroom soup
cooked rice or egg noodles

Heat oil in a Dutch oven over medium heat. Add onion, pepper, celery and chicken; cook until chicken juices run clear. While chicken is cooking, place sausage in a microwave-safe dish with just enough water to cover it. Cook for 5 minutes on high setting; drain sausage and add to chicken mixture. Add tomatoes; cook for 10 minutes over low heat. Add tomato paste and soup; stir until well blended. Simmer for 3 minutes, or until bubbly. Serve over hot rice or noodles. Makes 4 to 6 servings.

Cheesy Corn Muffins:
Prepare an 8-1/2 ounce package cornbread mix according to package directions. Stir in a 4-ounce can green chiles and 1/2 cup shredded Cheddar cheese. Pour into 6 to 10 greased muffin cups. Bake at 400 degrees, until a toothpick tests clean. Makes 6 to 10.

Peach Crème Brulée:
Place 2 cups canned sliced peaches in a lightly greased 8"x8" baking pan; spoon one cup sour cream over top. Sprinkle evenly with 1/2 cup brown sugar; broil until sugar melts and caramelizes. Serves 6.

Fire & Velvet Zingers

Jane Finn
Gurnee, IL

Just use mild sausage if you prefer a less spicy taste.

1 lb. hot ground pork sausage
1 onion, chopped
1 green pepper, chopped
8-oz. pkg. elbow macaroni,
    uncooked

14-oz. can crushed tomatoes
1 c. sour cream
1-1/4 c. milk
2 T. sugar
1 T. chili powder

Combine sausage, onion and pepper in a skillet over medium heat; cook until browned. Drain; stir in uncooked macaroni and remaining ingredients. Cover and simmer for 20 minutes, until macaroni is tender and mixture is still a little saucy. Serves 4.

Parmesan Asparagus:

Melt one tablespoon butter with 1/4 cup olive oil in a skillet over medium heat; add one pound trimmed asparagus spears. Cook, stirring occasionally, for about 10 minutes; drain. Sprinkle with 3/4 cup grated Parmesan cheese. Sprinkle with salt and pepper to taste. Serves 4.

Banana-Pineapple Toss:

Sprinkle 2 sliced bananas and 2 cups of pineapple chunks with amaretto cookie crumbs. Serves 4.

Post the day's dinner menu on a kitchen chalkboard.

Erin's Chicken Diane

Erin Siegrist
Erie, PA

Special enough for company.

2 T. butter
4 boneless, skinless chicken
    breasts
1/2 t. seasoning salt
1/4 t. pepper
1 t. dried parsley
1 clove garlic, minced

16-oz. pkg. sliced mushrooms
1/2 c. onion, sliced
10-3/4 oz. can cream of
    mushroom soup
1/2 c. milk
Garnish: 1 t. dried chives

Melt butter in a skillet over medium heat; add chicken. Sprinkle with seasoning salt, pepper and parsley. Cook until golden; turn over. Add garlic, mushrooms and onion; cook until chicken is cooked through. Remove chicken from skillet. Add soup and milk to skillet, stirring briskly until sauce is well blended. Return chicken to pan; heat through. Garnish with chives. Serves 4.

Roasted New Potatoes:

Toss 1-1/2 pounds halved new potatoes with 2 tablespoons olive oil. Sprinkle with salt and pepper. Bake at 450 degrees for about 30 minutes, until tender and golden. Serves 4.

Peanut Butter-Honey Dip:

Scoop 1/3 cup peanut butter into a small bowl; gradually stir in 2 tablespoons each of milk and honey. Add one tablespoon apple juice and cinnamon to taste. Stir in raisins, if desired. Serve with cut-up apples, pears and bananas as dippers. Serves 4.

Apples, bananas and tomatoes ripen quickly
if placed overnight in a brown paper bag.

Quick Cajun Shrimp

Stacie Mickley
Gooseberry Patch

*Purchase frozen, peeled shrimp
to make this meal even quicker.*

1/2 c. olive oil
2 T. Cajun seasoning
2 T. lemon juice
2 T. fresh parsley, chopped
1 T. honey
1 T. soy sauce

1/8 t. cayenne pepper
1 lb. uncooked large shrimp,
   cleaned and peeled
Garnish: grated Parmesan
   cheese

Combine first 7 ingredients in an ungreased 13"x9" baking pan.
Add shrimp; toss to coat. Bake at 450 degrees for 8 to 10 minutes,
until shrimp turn pink. Toss shrimp and pan juices with Pasta &
Peppers. Garnish with grated Parmesan cheese as desired.
Serves 4.

Pasta & Peppers:
Cook an 8-ounce package of favorite pasta according to package
directions. During last 4 minutes of cooking, stir in a 16-ounce bag
of frozen peppers and onions; drain. Sprinkle with salt, pepper and
grated Parmesan cheese. Serves 4.

Maple Ice Cream Sundaes:
Scoop vanilla ice cream into 4 serving glasses; drizzle with maple
syrup, a dash of cinnamon and toasted chopped walnuts. Serves 4.

Fill a big shaker with a favorite all-purpose spice
mixture...keep it by the stove for a dash of flavor
on meats and veggies as they cook.

Zesty Grilled Shrimp

Liz Gist
Orlando, FL

A delightful dinner for two, easily doubled for more.

1/4 c. oil
2 T. teriyaki sauce
juice of one lemon
1 T. garlic powder
2 t. paprika
2 t. dried cilantro

1/4 t. salt
1/4 t. pepper
1 lb. cooked small shrimp
1/4 c. sesame-ginger
    salad dressing
Optional: lemon slices

Mix together oil, sauce, juice and seasonings in a shallow dish; add shrimp. Marinate for 20 to 30 minutes. Grill on a preheated indoor countertop grill, or sauté in a lightly greased skillet, until heated through. Drizzle with salad dressing; garnish with lemon slices, if desired. Serves 2.

Oriental Cabbage Slaw:
Combine one cup shredded coleslaw mix with sesame-ginger salad dressing; stir in 1/3 cup mandarin oranges. Serves 2.

Coconut Pudding:
Prepare one small package instant coconut cream pudding mix according to package directions. Top with whipped topping; sprinkle with toasted coconut, if desired. Serves 2 to 4.

Take the kids along to a farmers' market.
Let each choose a favorite and help prepare it...
even picky eaters will want to eat their very own veggie.

Quick & Easy Spaghetti Toss

Sean Avner
Delaware, OH

Don't be afraid of the anchovies...they give this dish a delicious savory taste.

1-1/2 T. olive oil
3 cloves garlic, minced
6 anchovy fillets, minced
28-oz. can plum tomatoes
3.8-oz. can sliced black olives,
   drained
1/4 c. capers
8-oz. pkg. spaghetti, cooked
Garnish: grated Parmesan
   cheese, chopped fresh
   parsley

Heat oil in a large heavy skillet over medium heat; add garlic and anchovy fillets. Sauté until anchovies are almost dissolved; add tomatoes with juice, olives and capers. Cook for 5 minutes. Toss sauce over cooked spaghetti; mix well. Sprinkle with grated Parmesan and parsley. Serves 4 to 6.

Artichoke-Green Bean Salad:
Steam 1/2 pound green beans; cool. Combine with an 8-ounce jar of artichoke hearts in marinade. Sprinkle toasted, chopped walnuts over top of salad. Serves 4.

Apricot Fool:
Fold together a 21-ounce can of apricot pie filling and 2 cups thawed frozen whipped topping. Spoon into parfait glasses; sprinkle each with one tablespoon of toasted coconut. Serves 6.

The true essentials
of a feast are only
food and fun.

-Oliver Wendell Holmes, Sr.

Citrus-Grilled Pork Tenderloin

Jo Ann

Mmm...a family favorite!

1-lb. pork tenderloin, sliced
   3/4-inch thick
1/2 t. pepper
2/3 c. orange marmalade

1/4 c. fresh mint, chopped
1/4 c. soy sauce
4 cloves garlic, minced

Sprinkle pork slices with pepper. Combine remaining ingredients; stir well. Brush over pork, reserving remaining marmalade mixture. Place pork on a lightly greased grill over high heat; grill for 3 minutes per side, or until no longer pink. Baste frequently with reserved marmalade mixture. Place marmalade mixture in a saucepan and bring to a boil over medium heat; cook for one minute. Drizzle over pork. Serves 4.

Nectarine Coleslaw:
Combine 2 cups creamy deli coleslaw, one cup chopped nectarines and 1/4 cup honey-roasted peanuts. Toss gently to combine. Serves 4.

Creamy Chocolate Mousse:
Beat together one can sweetened condensed milk, a small package of instant chocolate pudding mix and one cup cold water; chill for 5 minutes. Fold in 2 cups thawed frozen whipped topping. Serves 4.

Keep kitchen scissors nearby...they make short work
of snipping fresh herbs, chopping green onions or even
cutting up whole tomatoes right in the can.

It's in the BAG!

One shopping list,
5 dinners

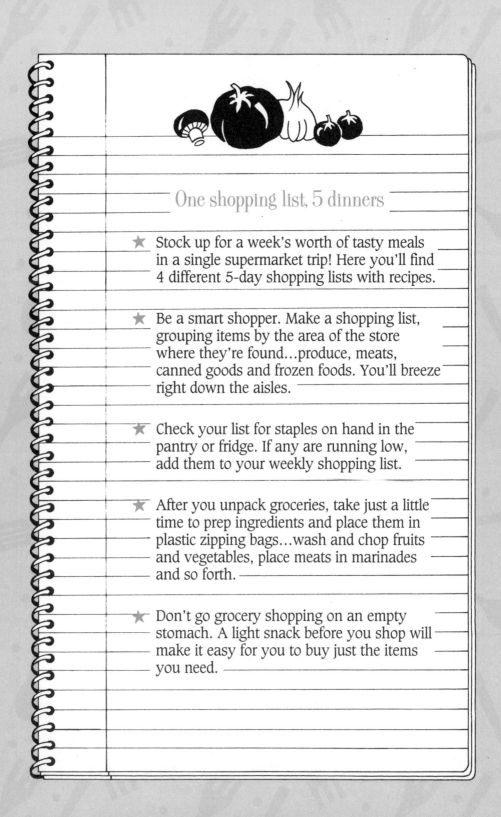

One shopping list, 5 dinners

★ Stock up for a week's worth of tasty meals in a single supermarket trip! Here you'll find 4 different 5-day shopping lists with recipes.

★ Be a smart shopper. Make a shopping list, grouping items by the area of the store where they're found...produce, meats, canned goods and frozen foods. You'll breeze right down the aisles.

★ Check your list for staples on hand in the pantry or fridge. If any are running low, add them to your weekly shopping list.

★ After you unpack groceries, take just a little time to prep ingredients and place them in plastic zipping bags...wash and chop fruits and vegetables, place meats in marinades and so forth.

★ Don't go grocery shopping on an empty stomach. A light snack before you shop will make it easy for you to buy just the items you need.

Week 1

MENU:

Citrus-Glazed Chicken
Beachfront Crab Cakes
Caribbean Chicken Salad
Gobblin' Good Turkey Burgers
Chinese Pepper Steak

Check the pantry for these items:

- [ ] oil
- [ ] butter
- [ ] salt & pepper
- [ ] cornstarch
- [ ] sugar
- [ ] eggs
- [ ] beef broth
- [ ] mayonnaise
- [ ] honey-mustard salad dressing

- [ ] rice wine vinegar
- [ ] Worcestershire sauce
- [ ] soy sauce
- [ ] minced garlic
- [ ] ground ginger
- [ ] dry mustard
- [ ] instant rice
- [ ] round buttery crackers

Shopping List:

- [ ] 10 boneless, skinless chicken breasts
- [ ] 1 lb. ground turkey
- [ ] 1 lb. beef sirloin
- [ ] 1 lb. crabmeat
- [ ] 8-oz. pkg. shredded Cheddar cheese
- [ ] 8-oz. bottle orange juice
- [ ] 2 oranges
- [ ] 1 lime
- [ ] 2 mangoes
- [ ] 2 10-oz. pkgs. mixed salad greens
- [ ] 3 onions

- [ ] 2 green peppers
- [ ] 2 bunches green onions
- [ ] 1 bunch fresh parsley
- [ ] Jamaican jerk seasoning
- [ ] 6 to 8 hamburger buns

Make copies of
this page for future use!

Citrus-Glazed Chicken

Marian Buckley
Fontana, CA

Sprinkle with chopped peanuts for a crunchy contrast.

6 boneless, skinless
   chicken breasts
1/2 t. salt
1/8 t. pepper

1 c. orange juice
3 T. butter
1 T. cornstarch

Sprinkle chicken breasts with salt and pepper; set aside. Stir together orange juice, butter and cornstarch in a small saucepan over medium heat until smooth. Cook, stirring constantly, until mixture thickens and comes to a full boil, 5 to 7 minutes. Heat a gas grill on medium. Place chicken on grill; brush with glaze. Grill for 12 to 15 minutes, until chicken juices run clear, turning once and brushing with glaze. Bring remaining glaze to a full boil; serve with chicken and Orange Salsa. Makes 6 servings.

Orange Salsa:

2 oranges, sectioned
   and chopped
2 T. green onion, sliced

2 T. fresh parsley, chopped
1 T. sugar

Stir together all salsa ingredients in a small bowl. Cover and chill until serving time.

Roll up sets of silverware in cloth napkins as you take it from the dishwasher...all ready for next mealtime!

It's in the Bag!

Beachfront Crab Cakes

Elizabeth Van Etten
Warwick, NY

These freeze well...just reheat on a baking sheet.

1 lb. crabmeat
1 egg, beaten
8 to 10 buttery round crackers,
    crushed
1/4 c. onion, diced

1/8 t. pepper
2 to 3 sprigs fresh parsley,
    minced
2 to 3 T. mayonnaise
oil for frying

Combine crabmeat, egg, crackers, onion, pepper and parsley in a
large bowl. Stir in mayonnaise; moisten hands with cold water and
mix well. Form into 3-inch patties. In a skillet, heat just enough oil
to cover crab cakes; fry on both sides until golden. Place on paper
towels to drain. Makes 4 servings.

Pick up some paper plates and cups in seasonal designs...
they'll make dinner fun even when you're in a hurry
and clean-up will be a breeze.

Caribbean Chicken Salad

Cheri Maxwell
Gulf Breeze, FL

Try grilling the chicken on a countertop grill for a different flavor.

1/2 c. honey-mustard
   salad dressing
1 t. lime zest
4 boneless, skinless chicken
   breasts
1 T. Jamaican jerk seasoning

1 T. oil
2 10-oz. pkgs. mixed
   salad greens
2 mangoes, peeled, pitted
   and diced

Stir together salad dressing and lime zest; cover and chill. Sprinkle chicken with seasoning. Heat oil over medium heat in a large skillet. Add chicken; cook 6 minutes per side until golden and no longer pink. Slice chicken thinly. Arrange salad greens on 4 plates; top with chicken and mangoes. Drizzle with dressing. Serves 4.

Greens will stay crisp if you start with less salad
dressing than you think you'll need...add
just enough to coat.

It's in the Bag!

Gobblin' Good Turkey Burgers

Brandi Glenn
Los Osos, CA

This was my mom's recipe...I'll take these over plain old hamburgers any day!

1 lb. ground turkey
1 onion, minced
1 c. shredded Cheddar cheese
1/4 c. Worcestershire sauce

1/2 t. dry mustard
salt and pepper to taste
6 to 8 hamburger buns, split

Combine all ingredients except buns; form into 4 to 6 patties. Grill to desired doneness; serve on hamburger buns. Makes 4 to 6 sandwiches.

Put a few extra burgers on the grill, then pop into buns, wrap individually and freeze. Later, just reheat in the microwave for quick meals...they'll taste freshly grilled!

Chinese Pepper Steak

Julee Wallberg
Reno, NV

It's a snap to slice the beef thinly if you place it in the freezer for 15 or 20 minutes first.

1-1/2 T. rice wine vinegar
2 T. soy sauce
1 clove garlic, minced
1 t. ground ginger
1 lb. beef sirloin, cut into
   thin strips
3 T. oil, divided

2 green peppers, cut into strips
1 onion, sliced
1 c. beef broth
1/4 t. pepper
2 t. cornstarch
1/4 c. water
cooked rice

Combine vinegar, soy sauce, garlic and ginger in a bowl; mix well. Add beef strips; toss to coat. Heat 1-1/2 tablespoons oil in a skillet over high heat. Add beef and stir-fry until meat is no longer red, 2 to 3 minutes. Remove beef to a plate. Heat remaining oil in skillet; stir-fry green peppers and onion until crisp-tender, 2 to 3 minutes. Return beef to skillet; add broth and pepper. Bring to a boil. Dissolve cornstarch in water; stir into beef mixture. Cook and stir over high heat until sauce boils and thickens, one to 2 minutes. Serve over cooked rice. Makes 4 servings.

Be sure to label any leftovers that are intended for future use...that way, Wednesday's supper won't turn into Tuesday's after-school snack!

Week 2

MENU:

Smothered Chicken
Shrimp & Mushroom Fettuccine
Grilled Gouda Sandwiches
Cheesy Chili Bake
Steak & Blue Cheese Quesadilla Salad

★

Check the pantry for these items:

- [ ] non-stick vegetable spray
- [ ] oil
- [ ] butter
- [ ] salt & pepper
- [ ] chicken broth
- [ ] Dijon mustard

- [ ] evaporated milk
- [ ] grated Parmesan cheese
- [ ] minced garlic
- [ ] cayenne pepper
- [ ] dry white wine
- [ ] fettuccine pasta

Week 2 Shopping List:

- [ ] 4 boneless, skinless chicken breasts
- [ ] 1 lb. ground beef
- [ ] 1/2 lb. beef flank steak
- [ ] 3/4 lb. large shrimp, peeled
- [ ] 8-oz. pkg. shredded Colby Jack cheese
- [ ] 1/2 lb. sliced Gouda cheese
- [ ] 4-oz. container blue cheese
- [ ] 8-oz. container sour cream
- [ ] 2 10-oz. pkgs. leaf lettuce
- [ ] 3 onions
- [ ] 1 red onion
- [ ] 1 green pepper
- [ ] 1 bunch celery
- [ ] 2 tomatoes

- [ ] 1 portabella mushroom
- [ ] 1 bunch fresh Italian parsley
- [ ] 1 bunch fresh chives
- [ ] 14-1/2 oz. can diced tomatoes with jalapeños
- [ ] 15-oz. can corn
- [ ] 15-oz. can kidney beans
- [ ] 16-oz. bottle favorite salad dressing
- [ ] 1-1/4 oz. pkg. chili seasoning mix
- [ ] 3/4-oz. pkg. mushroom gravy mix
- [ ] 10-oz. pkg. corn chips
- [ ] 1 pkg. 8-inch flour tortillas
- [ ] 1 loaf country-style bread

Smothered Chicken

Tori Willis
Champaign, IL

Serve with mashed potatoes...pure comfort food!

1 T. oil
1/4 c. onion, finely chopped
1/4 c. green pepper, finely
   chopped
1/4 c. celery, finely chopped

1 lb. boneless, skinless chicken
   breasts or thighs
3/4-oz. pkg. mushroom gravy
   mix
12-oz. can evaporated milk

Heat oil in a skillet. Sauté vegetables over medium-high heat for 2 minutes, or until crisp-tender. Add chicken; cook for 6 to 7 minutes per side until golden. Blend together gravy mix and milk; stir into skillet. Bring to a boil; reduce heat, cover and simmer for 15 minutes, until chicken juices run clear. To serve, spoon gravy from pan over chicken. Makes 4 servings.

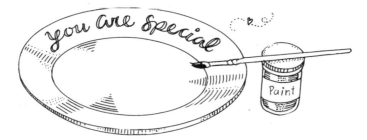

Create a family tradition of honoring birthdays, good report cards and other milestones. Look for a plate that says "You Are Special" or simply choose a brightly colored garage-sale find that stands out from the rest of your dinnerware.

It's in the Bag!

Shrimp & Mushroom Fettuccine

Diana Chaney
Olathe, KS

*I like to keep frozen packages of peeled, uncooked shrimp
on hand for quick, delicious meals...just thaw according
to package directions.*

1 T. olive oil
1 portabella mushroom, sliced
1 c. onion, finely chopped
1/4 c. Italian parsley, chopped
1/4 t. salt
1 clove garlic, minced
1 c. chicken broth

1/4 c. sherry or chicken broth
1 lb. uncooked large shrimp,
  peeled and cleaned
8-oz. pkg. fettuccine pasta,
  cooked
1/2 c. grated Parmesan cheese
1 T. fresh chives, chopped

Heat oil in a large saucepan over medium-high heat. Add
mushroom, onion, parsley, salt and garlic; sauté for 4 minutes,
or until mushroom releases moisture, stirring frequently. Stir in
broth, sherry or broth and shrimp; bring to a boil. Add fettuccine;
cook for 3 minutes, or until shrimp turn pink, tossing to combine.
Sprinkle with cheese and chives. Serves 4.

Steam veggies to keep their fresh-picked taste...it's easy!
Bring 1/2 inch of water to a boil in a saucepan and add cut-up
veggies. Cover and cook for 3 to 5 minutes, to desired tenderness.
A quick toss with a little butter and they're ready to enjoy.

Grilled Gouda Sandwiches

Tiffany Brinkley
Broomfield, CO

Good ol' grilled cheese, all grown up.

8 slices country-style bread
1 clove garlic, halved
4 t. Dijon mustard
1/2 lb. sliced Gouda cheese

2 T. butter, melted
1/8 t. cayenne pepper
1/8 t. pepper

Rub one side of each slice of bread with garlic. Place 4 bread slices garlic-side down; top each bread slice with one teaspoon mustard and 2 slices Gouda. Place remaining bread slices, garlic-side up, on sandwich bottoms. Combine butter, cayenne pepper and pepper in a small bowl; brush mixture over each side of sandwiches. Cook sandwiches in an oven-proof skillet over medium-high heat for about 2 minutes on each side, until golden. Place skillet in oven and bake at 400 degrees for about 5 minutes, until cheese is melted. Slice sandwiches diagonally. Makes 4 sandwiches.

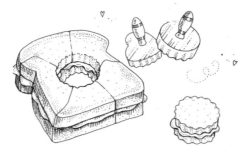

Delight finicky eaters with jigsaw puzzle sandwiches.
Press a cookie cutter straight down in the center of a
sandwich, then slice the outer part of sandwich into
3 or 4 pieces. It works great with grilled cheese or
even peanut butter & jelly!

It's in the Bag!

Cheesy Chili Bake

Kathy Huff
Kingsport, TN

*Try this using ground turkey, low-fat cheese, fat-free corn chips
and fat-free sour cream...I think it's just as tasty.*

1 lb. ground beef
1 c. onion, chopped
1-1/4 oz. pkg. chili seasoning
   mix
14-1/2 oz. can diced tomatoes
   with jalapeños
15-oz. can corn, drained

15-oz. can kidney beans,
   drained and rinsed
1 c. corn or tortilla chips,
   crushed
1 c. shredded Colby Jack cheese
Garnish: sour cream

Brown together ground beef and onion in a skillet; drain. Add
chili seasoning, tomatoes, corn and beans; heat until warmed
through, stirring occasionally. Spoon mixture into a lightly greased
8"x8" baking pan sprayed with non-stick vegetable spray. Top
with crushed chips and cheese. Bake at 350 degrees until cheese
is bubbly, about 20 minutes. Garnish with dollops of sour cream.
Serves 4 to 6.

A happy family is but an earlier heaven.

-Sir John Bowring

Steak & Blue Cheese Quesadilla Salad

Joshua Logan
Corpus Christi, TX

Thinly sliced avocado wedges would be a delicious addition.

1/2 lb. beef flank steak
1/4 t. salt
1/4 t. pepper
1/2 c. crumbled blue cheese
4 8-inch flour tortillas
1 head lettuce, torn

1 c. red onion, sliced
2 tomatoes, cut into 8 wedges
  each
favorite salad dressing to taste

Sprinkle steak with salt and pepper. Grill steak over a medium-hot grill for about 4 minutes on each side, or until done. Let stand for 5 minutes. Thinly slice steak diagonally across the grain; set aside. Sprinkle 1/4 cup cheese evenly over each of 2 tortillas. Divide steak evenly over cheese; top with remaining tortillas. Heat a lightly greased skillet over medium heat; cook quesadillas 4 minutes on each side, or until golden. Remove quesadillas from skillet; cut each into 8 wedges. Combine lettuce, onion and tomatoes in a large bowl; drizzle with dressing and toss well. Divide salad evenly among 4 plates; top each serving with 4 wedges. Serves 4.

Add variety and flavor to salads...combine red leaf lettuce,
romaine and even fresh herbs with iceberg lettuce.
Plan on about 2 cups greens per person.

Week 3

MENU:

Bacony Chicken
Salmon Patties
Lemony Pork Piccata
Asian Chicken Salad
Yummy Blue Cheese Burgers

Check the pantry for these items:

- ☐ olive oil
- ☐ butter
- ☐ salt & pepper
- ☐ all-purpose flour
- ☐ sugar
- ☐ eggs
- ☐ mayonnaise
- ☐ vinegar
- ☐ sherry or chicken broth

- ☐ minced garlic
- ☐ dried parsley
- ☐ dried basil
- ☐ dried rosemary
- ☐ dried tarragon
- ☐ lemon-pepper seasoning
- ☐ Optional: flavor enhancer
- ☐ round buttery crackers

Week 3 Shopping List:

- ☐ 8 to 9 boneless, skinless chicken breasts
- ☐ 2 lbs. ground beef
- ☐ 1-lb. pork tenderloin
- ☐ 1/2 lb. bacon
- ☐ 8-oz. pkg. shredded Cheddar cheese
- ☐ 4-oz. container blue cheese
- ☐ 6-oz. container plain yogurt
- ☐ 1/2 pt. half-and-half
- ☐ 1 head lettuce
- ☐ 1 bunch green onions
- ☐ 2 onions
- ☐ 1 cucumber

- ☐ 8-oz. pkg. sliced mushrooms
- ☐ 1/4 lb. snow peas
- ☐ 2 lemons
- ☐ 15-1/2 oz. can salmon
- ☐ 3-oz. jar capers
- ☐ poppy seed
- ☐ Cajun seasoning mix
- ☐ 2 T. slivered almonds
- ☐ 5-oz. can chow mein noodles
- ☐ 6 English muffins
- ☐ 6 kaiser rolls

Bacony Chicken

Annette Ingram
Grand Rapids, MI

Choose hickory-smoked bacon for extra flavor.

6 slices bacon, crisply cooked,
   crumbled and drippings
   reserved
1 T. butter
1 T. olive oil
6 boneless, skinless chicken
   breasts

1 onion, chopped
3 cloves garlic, minced
1/2 t. salt
1/8 t. pepper
1-1/2 c. shredded Cheddar
   cheese

Combine reserved drippings, butter and oil in a skillet over
medium heat. Add chicken and cook, turning once, until no
longer pink. Remove chicken from skillet; arrange in an ungreased
13"x9" baking pan. Set aside. Add onion and garlic to skillet;
cook until onion is soft. Stir in salt, pepper and crumbled bacon.
Spoon onion mixture over chicken; sprinkle with cheese. Bake at
350 degrees for 10 to 15 minutes, until cheese is melted. Serves 6.

Save bacon drippings in an empty jar in the fridge.
Add just a little to the oil when frying potatoes for
delicious country-style flavor.

It's in the Bag!

Salmon Patties

Carol Hickman
Kingsport, TN

*A delicious standby...so quick to fix, and most
of the ingredients are right in the cupboard.*

15-1/2 oz. can salmon, drained
   and flaked
1/2 c. round buttery crackers,
   crushed
1/2 T. dried parsley
1/2 t. lemon zest

1 T. lemon juice
2 green onions, sliced
1 egg, beaten
2 T. oil
5 to 6 English muffins, split
   and toasted

Combine first 7 ingredients; form into 5 to 6 patties. Heat oil
in a skillet over medium heat. Cook patties 4 to 5 minutes on
each side, until golden. Serve on English muffins topped with
Cucumber Sauce. Serves 5 to 6.

Cucumber Sauce:

1/3 c. cucumber, chopped
1/4 c. plain yogurt

1/4 c. mayonnaise
1/4 t. dried tarragon

Combine all ingredients; chill until ready to serve.

Whip up a tasty dip for sliced fruit.
Swirl fruit preserves into vanilla yogurt...just
the thing for hungry kids waiting for dinnertime.

Lemony Pork Piccata

Melody Taynor
Everett, WA

Serve over quick-cooking angel hair pasta to enjoy every drop of the savory sauce.

1-lb. pork tenderloin, sliced into 8 portions
3 T. all-purpose flour
2 t. lemon-pepper seasoning
2 t. butter

1/4 c. dry sherry or chicken broth
1/4 c. lemon juice
4 to 6 thin slices lemon
1/4 c. capers

Gently flatten pork slices to 1/8-inch thick. Lightly sprinkle with flour and seasoning. Melt butter in a large skillet over medium-high heat; add pork. Quickly sauté pork, turning once, until golden, about 3 to 4 minutes on each side. Remove pork to a serving plate; set aside. Add sherry or chicken broth and lemon juice to skillet. Cook for 2 minutes, scraping up browned bits, until slightly thickened. Add pork; heat through. Garnish with lemon slices and capers. Serves 4.

Turn fruit juice into a delicious beverage...add a splash of ginger ale and a skewer of fruit cubes lined up on a plastic straw.

Asian Chicken Salad

Tammy Rowe
Bellevue, OH

Another night, make lettuce wraps. Separate the lettuce into large leaves, layer with toppings and drizzle with dressing...wrap and eat.

1 head lettuce, shredded
2 to 3 boneless, skinless
   chicken breasts, cooked and
   shredded
1/2 c. snow peas

1 bunch green onions, chopped
2 T. slivered almonds
5-oz. can chow mein noodles
2 T. poppy seed

Combine all ingredients in a large salad bowl. Pour dressing over top and toss well. Serve immediately. Makes 4 servings.

Dressing:

1/4 c. vinegar
2 T. sugar
1/2 t. salt

1/2 t. pepper
Optional: 2 t. flavor enhancer

Whisk ingredients together until well combined.

Candlelight makes any family meal special.
Set lit votives on a footed cake stand
for a quick & easy centerpiece.

Yummy Blue Cheese Burgers

*Lynn Daniel
Portage, MI*

These mouthwatering burgers will be a hit at your next cookout.

2 lbs. ground beef
Cajun seasoning to taste
1 c. half-and-half
1 clove garlic, finely minced
1 t. dried rosemary
1 t. dried basil

4-oz. container crumbled
   blue cheese
6 kaiser rolls, split, toasted
   and buttered
Optional: sliced mushrooms,
   sliced onion, butter

Form ground beef into 6 patties; sprinkle with Cajun seasoning to taste. Grill to desired doneness. Combine half-and-half, garlic and herbs in a saucepan. Bring to a boil; simmer until thickened and reduced by half. Add blue cheese; stir just until melted. Place burgers on rolls; spoon sauce over burgers. If desired, sauté mushrooms and onion in butter until tender; spoon onto burgers. Serves 6.

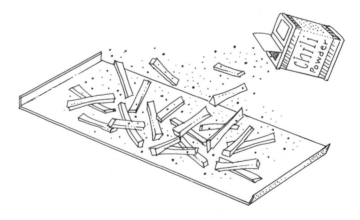

Spice up frozen French fries! Simply spritz with olive oil and sprinkle with chili powder before popping them in the oven.

Week 4

MENU:

Cider Mill Pork Chops & Noodles
Chicken & Sausage Skilletini
Spice-Rubbed Steak
Tarragon Steak Dinner Salad
Foil-Wrapped Baked Salmon

Check the pantry for these items:

- [ ] non-stick vegetable spray
- [ ] olive oil
- [ ] butter
- [ ] salt & pepper
- [ ] cornstarch
- [ ] brown sugar
- [ ] beef broth
- [ ] honey mustard
- [ ] dried thyme

- [ ] minced garlic
- [ ] dried oregano
- [ ] dried basil
- [ ] garlic powder
- [ ] onion powder
- [ ] paprika
- [ ] 2 T. red wine
- [ ] wide egg noodles

Week 4 Shopping List:

- [ ] 1/2 lb. beef sirloin
- [ ] 1 to 1-1/2 lb. beef strip steak
- [ ] 4 boneless pork loin chops
- [ ] 4 salmon fillets
- [ ] 2 boneless, skinless chicken breasts
- [ ] 1/2 lb. spicy ground pork sausage
- [ ] 1/2 lb. bacon
- [ ] 4-oz. container blue cheese
- [ ] 1 pt. apple cider
- [ ] 2 pears
- [ ] 1 lemon

- [ ] 1 head Boston lettuce
- [ ] 8-oz. pkg. sliced mushrooms
- [ ] 2 red onions
- [ ] 2 onions
- [ ] 1 red pepper
- [ ] 2 shallots
- [ ] 1 bunch fresh tarragon
- [ ] 9-oz. pkg. frozen green beans
- [ ] 14-1/2 oz. can diced tomatoes
- [ ] 16-oz. pkg. linguine pasta
- [ ] 8-oz. bottle red wine vinaigrette salad dressing

Cider Mill Pork Chops & Noodles

Jonnah Rix
Marion, IL

A luscious, tender meal-in-one.

2-1/2 c. extra wide egg noodles, uncooked
9-oz. pkg. frozen green beans
3 slices bacon, crisply cooked and crumbled, drippings reserved
4 boneless pork loin chops
1/4 c. onion, chopped

1 c. apple cider
1 t. honey mustard
1/4 t. salt
1/8 t. pepper
1/4 t. dried thyme
1 T. cold water
1 T. cornstarch

Cook noodles according to package directions, adding green beans during last 4 minutes. Drain; cover to keep warm and set aside. Heat drippings in a skillet. Add pork chops; sprinkle onion around chops. Cook 3 to 5 minutes, until chops are golden, turning once. In a small bowl, combine cider, mustard, salt, pepper and thyme; mix well and pour over chops. Reduce heat to low; cover and cook for 10 to 15 minutes, until chops are cooked through. In another small bowl, mix together water and cornstarch until smooth. Add to juices in skillet; mix well. Cook over medium-low until bubbly and thickened; simmer for one minute. Arrange chops over noodle mixture. Spoon gravy over top; sprinkle with crumbled bacon. Serves 4.

After cutting onions, dip a lemon wedge into salt and rub over your hands...rinse under cool water for sweet-smelling hands.

It's in the Bag!

Chicken & Sausage Skilletini

Elizabeth Cisneros
Chino Hills, CA

*I like to serve this hearty one-pan dish with French bread
and olive oil for dipping.*

1/4 c. olive oil
2 boneless, skinless chicken
   breasts, cubed
1/2 lb. spicy ground pork
   sausage
1 red onion, thinly sliced
2 cloves garlic, minced
14-1/2 oz. can diced tomatoes

1 red pepper, sliced
3 T. brown sugar, packed
1/2 t. dried oregano
1 t. dried basil
1/8 t. salt
1/8 t. pepper
16-oz. pkg. linguine pasta,
   cooked

Heat oil in a large skillet over medium heat. Add chicken,
sausage, onion and garlic; cook until chicken and sausage are
cooked through. Add remaining ingredients except pasta; simmer
for 5 minutes. Add cooked pasta to skillet; simmer for an
additional 5 minutes. Serves 4 to 6.

It just wouldn't be dinner without dessert. Dress up bakery
pound cake with a spoonful of cherry pie filling and a dollop
of whipped topping...almost as good as homemade!

Spice-Rubbed Steak

Samantha Starks
Madison, WI

Pair with baked sweet potatoes for a memorable meal.

2 t. paprika
1 t. salt
1 t. pepper
1/2 t. garlic powder
1/2 t. onion powder
1/2 t. dried thyme

1 to 1-1/2 lb. beef strip steak
2 T. butter
1/4 c. shallots, minced
8-oz. pkg. sliced mushrooms
2 T. red wine or beef broth
1 T. oil

Mix together seasonings; sprinkle on both sides of steak and set aside. Melt butter in a large skillet over medium heat. Add shallots; cook for one minute. Add mushrooms and cook for 2 to 3 minutes, until tender. Stir in wine or broth; cook until most of liquid has evaporated. Remove from heat; keep warm. Heat oil in a separate skillet over medium-high heat. Add steak; cook for 5 to 7 minutes per side, or to desired doneness. Remove to a plate and let stand several minutes. Cut into serving-size portions and spoon mushroom mixture over top. Serves 3 to 4.

Buttery sweet corn is so delicious in the summer...why not enjoy it more often? Place 3 tablespoons melted butter in a microwave-safe dish, add 4 ears corn and roll to coat. Cover with plastic wrap and microwave on high for 6 to 8 minutes.

It's in the Bag!

Tarragon Steak Dinner Salad

Amanda Homan
Gooseberry Patch

Delicious...a perfect light summer meal.

6 c. Boston lettuce
2 pears, cored, peeled and sliced
1/2 red onion, thinly sliced
1/2 lb. grilled beef steak, thinly
    sliced

1/4 c. crumbled blue cheese
1/2 c. red wine vinaigrette
    salad dressing
1 T. fresh tarragon, minced
1/4 t. pepper

Arrange lettuce, pears and onion on 4 serving plates. Top with sliced steak and sprinkle with cheese. Combine dressing, tarragon and pepper in a small bowl; whisk well. Drizzle dressing mixture over salad. Serves 4.

Keep a notepad on the fridge to make a note
whenever a pantry staple is used up...
you'll never run out of that one item you need.

Foil-Wrapped Baked Salmon

Katherine Murnane
Plattsburgh, NY

These packets can also be cooked on a hot grill.

4 salmon fillets
1 onion, sliced
1/4 c. butter, diced

1 lemon, thinly sliced
1/4 c. brown sugar, packed

Place each fillet on a piece of aluminum foil that has been sprayed with non-stick vegetable spray. Top fillets evenly with onion slices, diced butter, lemon slices and brown sugar. Fold aluminum foil over tightly to make packets; make a few holes in top of packets with a fork to allow steam to escape. Arrange packets on an ungreased baking sheet. Bake at 375 degrees for 15 to 20 minutes. Serves 4.

Slip your hands inside 2 plastic bags when shaping ground beef into burgers...no more messy hands!

Cook once, Eat twice

Turn leftovers into plan-overs

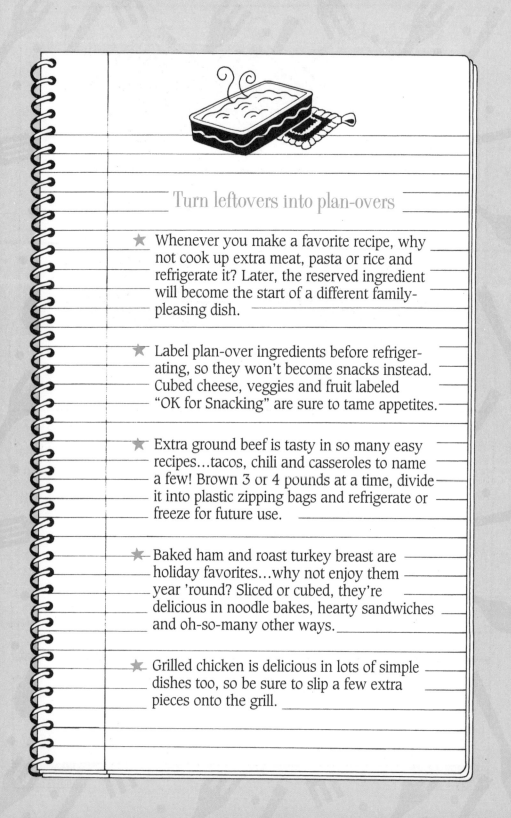

Turn leftovers into plan-overs

★ Whenever you make a favorite recipe, why not cook up extra meat, pasta or rice and refrigerate it? Later, the reserved ingredient will become the start of a different family-pleasing dish.

★ Label plan-over ingredients before refrigerating, so they won't become snacks instead. Cubed cheese, veggies and fruit labeled "OK for Snacking" are sure to tame appetites.

★ Extra ground beef is tasty in so many easy recipes...tacos, chili and casseroles to name a few! Brown 3 or 4 pounds at a time, divide it into plastic zipping bags and refrigerate or freeze for future use.

★ Baked ham and roast turkey breast are holiday favorites...why not enjoy them year 'round? Sliced or cubed, they're delicious in noodle bakes, hearty sandwiches and oh-so-many other ways.

★ Grilled chicken is delicious in lots of simple dishes too, so be sure to slip a few extra pieces onto the grill.

Cook once, Eat twice

Favorite Pineapple-Glazed Ham

Chrissy Walker
Mount Hermon, KY

Delicious enough for a holiday meal...too delicious not to eat more often!

5 to 6-lb. fully-cooked ham
8-oz. can lemon-lime soda
1-1/2 c. orange juice
1 c. pineapple juice
1 c. brown sugar, packed

3 T. honey
2 T. mustard
20-oz. can pineapple slices,
   drained

Place ham in an ungreased roasting pan; set aside. Mix remaining ingredients except pineapple slices in a large bowl; pour over ham. Arrange pineapple slices on ham and secure with toothpicks. Cover with aluminum foil; bake at 350 degrees for 3 hours. Let stand for a few minutes before slicing. Makes 12 to 15 servings.

Plan-Over Instructions:

Prepare a 6-pound ham. Reserve 6 serving-size ham slices for Ham & Sweet Potato Casserole on page 60 and 1-1/2 cups ham cubes for Hawaiian Ham Stir-Fry on page 61.

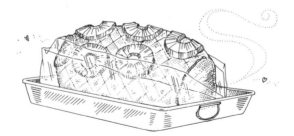

Oven roasting bags speed up the baking time for ham, pot roast and turkey. Clean-up is a breeze too... just toss away the mess.

Ham & Sweet Potato Casserole

Kathy Grashoff
Fort Wayne, IN

A scrumptious change from ham and scalloped white potatoes.

1-1/2 lbs. cooked ham,
   cut into 6 serving-size
   portions
1 T. oil

3 sweet potatoes, peeled and
   sliced
3 T. brown sugar, packed
1-1/2 c. hot water

In a skillet, brown ham in oil over medium heat; reserve drippings in skillet. Arrange ham in a 3-quart casserole dish; top with sweet potatoes. Sprinkle with brown sugar and set aside. Add hot water to drippings in skillet; cook and stir. Pour over sweet potatoes. Cover and bake at 350 degrees for 45 minutes, basting with pan drippings after 20 minutes. Uncover and bake an additional 15 minutes, until golden. Makes 6 servings.

No peeking when there's a casserole in the oven!
Every time the oven door is opened, the temperature drops
at least 25 degrees...dinner will take longer to bake.

Hawaiian Ham Stir-Fry

Lynn Williams
Muncie, IN

Tasty sprinkled with toasted sesame seed and green onion.

20-oz. can pineapple chunks,
    drained and juice reserved
2 T. orange juice
2 T. vinegar
2 T. soy sauce
1 T. cornstarch
1/4 t. garlic powder

1/4 t. red pepper flakes
1/4 t. ground ginger
1 T. oil
16-oz. pkg. frozen stir-fry
    vegetables
1-1/2 c. cooked ham, cubed
3 c. cooked rice

Stir together reserved pineapple juice, orange juice, vinegar, soy sauce, cornstarch and seasonings; set aside. Heat oil in a large skillet over medium-high heat; add vegetables and cook until tender. Add sauce mixture; cook and stir until thickened. Add ham and reserved pineapple; stir until heated through. Serve over hot cooked rice. Serves 4.

Bake up a quiche with leftover ham, chopped veggies and cheese! Put about a cup of ingredients in a pie crust, then whisk together 3 eggs and a small can of evaporated milk. Pour into crust and bake at 400 degrees until set, 20 to 25 minutes. Scrumptious any time of day!

Nacho Grande Casserole

Carol Hickman
Kingsport, TN

Hearty and satisfying.

2 lbs. ground beef
1 onion, chopped
16-oz. can tomato sauce
2 16-oz. cans spicy chili
   beans
1-1/4 oz. pkg. taco seasoning
   mix
16-oz. pkg. frozen corn,
   thawed

8-oz. pkg. finely
   shredded Cheddar Jack
   cheese, divided
9-oz. pkg. nacho cheese
   tortilla chips, crushed
   and divided
Optional: sour cream, chopped
   tomato and green onion

Brown ground beef and onion in a Dutch oven; drain. Add tomato sauce, beans, seasoning mix and corn; stir until blended. Simmer over medium heat for 10 minutes. Pour half of beef mixture into a 13"x9" baking pan lightly sprayed with non-stick vegetable spray. Top with half each of the cheese and crushed chips; repeat layers. Bake at 350 degrees for 25 to 30 minutes, until bubbly and golden. Top portions with a dollop of sour cream and a sprinkling of tomatoes and green onion, if desired. Makes 8 to 10 servings.

Plan-Over Instructions:
Brown a total of 3 pounds ground beef with onion as directed. Drain; reserve one-third for Pizzeria Bake on page 63.

For an oh-so cheerful table centerpiece, float 2 or
3 bright Gerbera daisies in a water-filled clear glass bowl.

Pizzeria Bake

LuAnn Trumpower
Mansfield, OH

I can't remember where I first got this recipe, but it has been a big hit with my family for many years now.

1 lb. ground beef, browned
   and drained
3 c. shredded mozzarella cheese,
   shredded and divided
2 c. cooked elbow macaroni

14-oz. jar mushroom
   spaghetti sauce
1 c. grated Parmesan cheese
3-1/2 oz. pkg. pepperoni,
   chopped

Mix together ground beef, one cup mozzarella cheese and remaining ingredients. Spread mixture in a lightly greased 13"x 9" baking pan; top with remaining cheese. Bake at 350 degrees for 30 to 35 minutes. Serves 6 to 8.

For the freshest flavor, keep olive oil in the fridge...just pour a little into a small bottle for everyday use. Oil may thicken when chilled, but will thin quickly at room temperature.

Chicken Ranch Jack

Sheila Wintermantel
Wellsville, OH

Grill the chicken strips instead of frying, if you prefer...and use chipotle-flavored ranch salad dressing for extra kick.

3 boneless, skinless chicken
   breasts, cut into strips
2 to 3 T. butter
1/4 c. ranch salad dressing

6 slices bacon, crisply cooked
   and crumbled
1/3 c. shredded Monterey
   Jack cheese

In a skillet over medium heat, sauté chicken strips in butter until cooked through. Turn into a lightly greased 2-quart casserole dish. Pour dressing over chicken; stir well. Sprinkle with bacon and cheese; broil until cheese is melted and golden. Makes 4 servings.

Plan-Over Instructions:

Sauté a total of 5 to 6 boneless chicken breasts, cut into strips. Reserve half for Grilled BBQ Chicken Pizza on page 65.

Whip up a cool fruit dessert...you won't believe how easy it is. Freeze an unopened can of your favorite fruit. At serving time, scoop out frozen fruit and process in a food processor until smooth.

Cook once, Eat twice

Grilled BBQ Chicken Pizza

Phyllis Wittig
Quartz Hill, CA

With the chicken already cooked, this goes together really fast.

13.8-oz. tube refrigerated
  pizza dough
1 c. barbecue sauce
2 boneless, skinless chicken
  breasts, cooked and cut
  into strips

8-oz. pkg. shredded
  mozzarella cheese
1/2 c. green onion, chopped

Spray a baking sheet with non-stick vegetable spray; lay out dough according to package directions. Spread sauce over dough; arrange cooked chicken strips on top. Sprinkle with shredded cheese. Spray cold grill with non-stick vegetable spray; preheat grill. Carefully lift dough off baking sheet onto grill; grill over low heat for 10 minutes. Use a spatula to remove pizza from grill; sprinkle with green onion. Slice into squares. Serves 4.

Let your grill do double duty...roast veggies alongside the meat. Brush sliced squash, potatoes, peppers or eggplant with olive oil and grill until tender. They're delicious warm or cold, so be sure to grill plenty for sides now and salads later.

Homestyle Pot Roast

Jody Bolen
Ashland, OH

This roast always turns out juicy and tender...
it makes its own gravy as it bakes.

1-1/2 oz. pkg. beefy onion
   soup mix
1-3/4 c. water
1/3 c. catsup
1/8 t. pepper
1 bay leaf

1/3 c. all-purpose flour
3 to 5-lb. beef chuck roast
4 to 6 potatoes, peeled and
   halved
4 carrots, peeled and sliced
3 stalks celery, sliced

Combine soup mix, water, catsup, pepper and bay leaf; stir well and set aside. Shake flour in a large oven roasting bag; place bag in a 13"x9" baking pan. Place roast in bag; arrange vegetables on top. Pour soup mixture over top. Close bag with nylon tie provided; cut six, 1/2-inch slits in top. Bake at 325 degrees for 2-1/2 to 3 hours. Discard bay leaf. Serve roast and vegetables with gravy from roasting bag. Makes 4 to 6 servings.

Plan-Over Instructions:

Bake a 5 to 6-pound chuck roast. Reserve 1-1/2 cups diced roast beef for Easy Beefy Pot Pie on page 67.

The feeling of friendship is like that of being
comfortably filled with roast beef.

-Samuel Johnson

Cook once, Eat twice

Easy Beefy Pot Pie

Sherry Gordon
Arlington Heights, IL

Substitute leftover cooked vegetables for the potatoes and mixed veggies...it's a great way to use them up.

1-1/2 c. roast beef, diced
2 c. potatoes, peeled, diced and cooked
10-oz. pkg. frozen mixed vegetables, thawed
10-3/4 oz. can golden mushroom soup

1/3 c. water
1 t. Worcestershire sauce
1 t. dried thyme
1 pie crust, unbaked

Arrange beef, potatoes and vegetables in a greased 1-1/2 quart casserole dish; set aside. Stir together soup, water, sauce and thyme in a medium bowl; pour over beef mixture. Gently place crust over beef mixture. Crimp edges of crust, sealing to dish; cut slits to vent. Bake at 400 degrees for 35 minutes, or until crust is golden. Serves 4.

Make mini pot pies! Spoon filling into oven-safe bowls and cut crust circles to fit, using another bowl as a guide. Set on a baking sheet. Bake for 20 to 25 minutes at 400 degrees, until bubbly and golden.

Spaghetti Pie

Susann Kropp
Cairo, NY

A fun way to eat spaghetti...kids love it!

8-oz. pkg. spaghetti, cooked
4 eggs, beaten and divided
2/3 c. grated Parmesan cheese
2 c. cottage cheese, drained
1 lb. ground beef

1 c. green pepper, chopped
1 c. onion, chopped
1-1/2 c. spaghetti sauce
1 c. shredded mozzarella
  cheese

Combine spaghetti with 2 eggs and Parmesan cheese; spread in a lightly greased 9" pie plate. Combine cottage cheese and remaining eggs; spread over spaghetti. Brown ground beef, green pepper and onion over medium heat; drain. Stir sauce into beef mixture; spread over top. Bake at 350 degrees for 30 minutes. Top with mozzarella cheese and bake an additional 5 minutes, or until cheese is melted. Cut into wedges to serve. Makes 4 to 6 servings.

Plan-Over Instructions:
Cook a 16-ounce package of spaghetti; drain. Toss half of spaghetti with a little oil and reserve for Mom's White Spaghetti on page 69, reheating at serving time.

It's easy to save leftover fresh herbs. Spoon chopped herbs into an ice cube tray, one tablespoon per cube. Cover with water and freeze. Frozen cubes can be dropped right into hot stew or soup.

Cook once, Eat twice

Mom's White Spaghetti

Sarah Weber
Colorado Springs, CO

I've had this recipe ever since I can remember. My mother couldn't eat tomatoes, so she came up with this recipe. Now I fix it for my own family.

2 T. oil
10-oz. pkg. frozen chopped
   spinach, thawed and drained
1 t. garlic, minced
1/2 c. water
1 T. chicken bouillon granules

1/2 t. dried basil
1/2 t. salt
1 c. large-curd cottage cheese
1/4 c. grated Parmesan cheese
8-oz. pkg. spaghetti, cooked

Heat oil in a large skillet over medium heat; add spinach and garlic. Sauté for 5 minutes. Add water, bouillon, basil and salt. Reduce heat; cover and cook until heated through. Remove from heat; stir in cheeses and toss with hot cooked spaghetti. Serves 4.

Kids love to "cook" so let them take turns selecting and helping prepare dinner at least once a week. Even if they choose PB&J sandwiches or boxed mac & cheese, they'll be learning basic kitchen skills.

Now & Later Chili Mac

Peggy Donnally
Toledo, OH

*This chili freezes well...cool and freeze in a
plastic freezer bag for a fast future dinner.*

3 lbs. ground beef
2 T. ground cumin
salt and pepper to taste
2 c. water
4 15-1/2 oz. cans mild chili
   beans in chili sauce
2 15-1/2 oz. cans hot chili
   beans in chili sauce

2 15-1/2 oz. cans dark red
   kidney beans, drained
   and rinsed
8-oz. pkg. angel hair pasta,
   cooked
Optional: shredded Cheddar
   cheese, diced onion

Brown beef over medium heat in a large stockpot until no longer
pink; drain. Stir in cumin, salt and pepper. Add water and beans;
cover and simmer for one hour, stirring occasionally. Divide
cooked pasta among 4 plates and ladle chili over each. Garnish
with cheese and onion, if desired. Makes 4 servings.

Plan-Over Instructions:

Prepare recipe as directed. Reserve 4 cups chili for South-of-the-
Border Taco Salad on page 71.

Cool coleslaw is always a welcome partner to spicy dishes.
Mix up bagged shredded cabbage mix with bottled
coleslaw dressing to taste, then make it special with diced
apple or even crumbled blue cheese. Ready in a wink!

Cook once, Eat twice

South-of-the-Border Taco Salad

Sarah Oravecz
Gooseberry Patch

A family favorite that's ready to serve in a jiffy.

4 c. prepared chili
6-oz. pkg. tortilla chips
4 c. romaine lettuce, shredded
4 c. iceberg lettuce, torn
8-oz. pkg. shredded Colby-Jack
   cheese

1 c. tomato, chopped
1 avocado, pitted, peeled
   and chopped
1/3 c. sour cream
1/2 c. salsa

Simmer chili in a saucepan over medium heat until hot and
bubbly. Arrange tortilla chips on 4 to 6 plates; top with lettuce.
Ladle chili over lettuce and top with remaining ingredients.
Makes 4 to 6 servings.

Fill a muffin tin with fixings like sliced black olives,
chopped green onion and diced avocado...everyone
can top their own taco salad to their liking.

Lemon Grove Chicken

Penny Sherman
Cumming, GA

Serve with steamed broccoli and rice for a complete meal.

1-1/4 lbs. boneless, skinless
   chicken breasts
1/4 c. all-purpose flour
1/2 t. pepper

1 T. oil
1 c. chicken broth
2 t. salt-free herb seasoning
2 T. lemon juice

Lightly coat chicken with flour; sprinkle with pepper. Heat oil in a skillet over medium-high heat. Add chicken; sauté 3 to 4 minutes per side, or until golden. Add broth and seasoning; cover and simmer for 10 minutes, until chicken juices run clear. Arrange chicken on a serving dish; set aside. Bring broth in skillet to a boil; cook and stir until slightly thickened. Stir in lemon juice; spoon sauce over chicken. Makes 4 servings.

Plan-Over Instructions:

Double chicken and all ingredients except lemon juice; sauté and simmer chicken as directed. Reduce liquid in skillet to one cup before adding lemon juice. Reserve 3 cups shredded chicken for Favorite Chicken & Noodles on page 73.

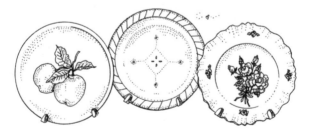

Watch for vintage plates at yard sales...they'll make fun conversation pieces at the family dinner table.

Favorite Chicken Noodle Bake

Lora Wells
West Jefferson, OH

My family really enjoys this simple dish.

3 c. cooked chicken, shredded
2 10-3/4 oz. cans cream of
   mushroom soup
1-1/4 c. milk
10-oz. pkg. frozen peas

16-oz. pkg. frozen wide
   egg noodles, cooked
1 sleeve round buttery
   crackers, crushed

In an ungreased 2-quart casserole dish, mix together shredded chicken, soup, milk and peas. Add noodles; stir to coat. Bake at 350 degrees for 30 minutes. Sprinkle with cracker crumbs and bake for an additional 5 minutes. Serves 4 to 6.

Bake a peach cobbler alongside tonight's dinner...it's so easy. Blend one cup sugar and 1/2 cup butter in a 9"x9" baking pan. Stir in one cup each of self-rising flour and milk and pour a 15-ounce can of peaches over top, juice and all. Bake at 350 degrees for 25 to 30 minutes, until golden. Mmm!

Herb Garden Turkey Breast

Wendy Jacobs
Idaho Falls, ID

Even more delicious made with fresh thyme and sage...just double the amounts called for.

8-1/2 lb. turkey breast
3 T. lemon juice, divided
2 T. oil, divided
2 cloves garlic, minced
1 t. lemon zest

1 t. dried thyme
1/2 t. dried sage
1-1/4 t. salt
3/4 t. pepper

Place turkey breast on a rack in an ungreased shallow roasting pan; loosen skin without removing it. Combine one tablespoon lemon juice, one tablespoon oil, garlic. zest and seasonings; spread under loosened skin. Combine remaining lemon juice and oil; set aside. Bake, uncovered, at 350 degrees for 2-1/2 to 3 hours, basting every 15 to 20 minutes with lemon mixture. Turkey is done when a meat thermometer inserted into thickest part reads 170 degrees. Remove to a serving platter; let stand for 10 minutes before slicing. Makes 14 to 16 servings.

Plan-Over Instructions:
Roast turkey as directed. Reserve 3 cups cubed turkey for California Cobb Salad on page 75.

Layer slices of leftover roast turkey over stuffing or mashed potatoes, ladle turkey gravy over the top and freeze...perfect for lunches or dinners on the go. Just microwave for a few minutes, until piping hot.

California Cobb Salad

Carrie O'Shea
Marina Del Rey, CA

Always popular at luncheons...simply arrange the ingredients in attractive rows on a single large platter.

1 head lettuce, shredded
3 c. cooked turkey, cubed
8 slices bacon, crisply cooked
    and crumbled
3 eggs, hard-boiled, peeled
    and sliced
2 tomatoes, chopped

1 avocado, pitted, peeled
    and diced
3/4 c. crumbled blue cheese
1 c. green onion, chopped
8-oz. bottle ranch salad
    dressing

Divide lettuce among 4 to 6 salad plates. Arrange remaining ingredients except dressing in rows over lettuce. Drizzle with dressing to taste. Makes 4 to 6 servings.

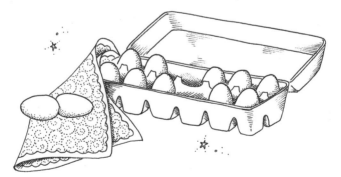

Here's a quick tip for bacon. Arrange slices on a baking sheet and bake at 350 degrees. It'll be crispy in about 15 minutes...no messy spatters!

Pepper Steak

Jill Valentine
Jackson, TN

*An old favorite! The recipe may look complicated
but it goes together quickly.*

2 t. cornstarch
1 T. cold water
3/4 c. chicken broth
2-1/2 T. dry sherry or
   chicken broth
2-1/2 T. oil
4 cloves garlic, pressed
4 to 6 slices fresh ginger, peeled
1 c. green pepper, sliced

1/2 c. onion, sliced
4-oz. can sliced mushrooms,
   drained
8-oz. can sliced water
   chestnuts, drained
1-lb. beef flank steak
salt and pepper to taste
cooked rice
Optional: soy sauce

Mix cornstarch and water in a small bowl; whisk in broth and
sherry or broth and set aside. Heat oil in a skillet over medium-
low heat. Sauté garlic and ginger until golden; discard garlic and
ginger, reserving oil in skillet. Add pepper, onion and mushrooms;
sauté until tender. Stir in water chestnuts and cornstarch mixture;
simmer until thickened. Sprinkle steak with salt and pepper; broil
4 inches from heat to desired doneness. Thinly slice steak on the
diagonal; add to vegetable mixture and heat through. Serve over
cooked rice, with soy sauce, as desired. Makes 4 servings.

Plan-Over Instructions:

Broil a 2-pound flank steak as directed. Reserve 2 cups diced beef
for Steakhouse Sandwiches on page 77.

Do some family members need to dash off to soccer practice
before dessert is served? They needn't miss out...spoon
single servings of dessert into mini cups and refrigerate,
to be enjoyed when they return home.

Steakhouse Sandwiches

John Alexander
New Britain, CT

*Serve in napkin-lined burger baskets with a side of
potato chips for a quick and delicious meal.*

2 c. cooked beef flank steak,
  diced
5 T. mayonnaise, divided
1 T. Dijon mustard
2 T. red onion, chopped
2 T. dill pickle, chopped

salt and pepper to taste
8 thick slices country-style
  bread
4 leaves romaine lettuce
1 tomato, cut into 8 slices

Combine steak, 2 tablespoons mayonnaise, mustard, onion and
pickle in a medium bowl. Toss to blend; add salt and pepper.
Spread bread slices on one side with remaining mayonnaise.
Divide steak mixture among 4 slices bread; top each with a lettuce
leaf, 2 tomato slices and a second slice of bread, mayonnaise-side
down. Slice sandwiches diagonally. Makes 4 sandwiches.

Crispy potato pancakes are a great way to use extra
mashed potatoes. Stir an egg yolk and some minced onion
into 2 cups potatoes. Form into patties and fry in butter
until golden. Delicious with grilled sausage.

Hearty Chicken & Noodles

Stephanie Moon
Nampa, ID

This is sooo good...real comfort food.

4 boneless, skinless chicken
    breasts
2 c. chicken broth
2 c. water
1/3 c. celery leaves, chopped
2 T. fresh parsley, chopped
1 t. salt
1/4 t. pepper
1/2 t. dried thyme
1/2 t. garlic powder

1/4 t. poultry seasoning
1 bay leaf
1 c. celery, chopped
2 c. carrots, peeled and sliced
3 c. wide egg noodles,
    uncooked
1 c. frozen peas
2 c. milk, divided
4 T. all-purpose flour

Combine chicken, broth, water, celery leaves and seasonings in a large Dutch oven; bring to a boil. Reduce heat to low; cover and simmer for 25 minutes. Add celery and carrots; cover and simmer for 20 minutes, until tender. Remove chicken and cool slightly, reserving broth in pan. Cube chicken and set aside. Discard bay leaf. Bring reserved broth to a boil; add noodles and simmer for 5 minutes. Stir in peas and 1-1/2 cups milk. Whisk together remaining milk and flour; stir into broth. Cook and stir until bubbly and thickened; stir in chicken. Stir in chicken and heat through. Makes 6 servings.

Plan-Over Instructions:

Simmer a total of 7 boneless chicken breasts as directed, adding more water to cover if necessary. Reserve half of cubed chicken for Chicken in a Cloud on page 79.

Keep a jar of minced garlic on hand for speedy suppers.
One-half teaspoon equals a clove of garlic.

Chicken in a Cloud

Debbie Moffatt
Prospect, PA

I use instant mashed potatoes to whip this up quickly.
Sometimes I'll top it with 2 cups shredded Cheddar or
Swiss cheese instead of the stuffing.

4 c. mashed potatoes
1-oz. pkg. ranch salad
   dressing mix
4.3-oz. pkg. chicken-flavor
   noodle & sauce mix,
   prepared

3 boneless, skinless chicken
   breasts, cooked and cubed
6-oz. pkg. stuffing mix,
   prepared

Combine potatoes and salad dressing mix; mix well. Spoon into
a greased 13"x9" baking pan, mounding around the edges; set
aside. Mix together noodles and chicken; pour over potato
mixture. Sprinkle with stuffing; bake at 350 degrees for 20 to
30 minutes, or until golden. Let stand for 5 minutes before
serving. Makes 6 to 8 servings.

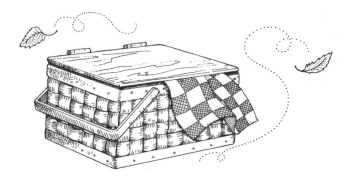

Make family dinners memorable! Eat in an unexpected
place like the backyard, the living room or even pack up
everything and go to a nearby park.

Charmie's Meatball Supper Soup

Charmie Fisher
Fontana, CA

This is my favorite soup... I developed it from a very old recipe.

10-1/2 oz. can beef broth
28-oz. can diced tomatoes in
   purée
2 c. carrots, peeled and sliced
2 c. potatoes, peeled and diced
1/4 c. celery, chopped
1/4 c. fresh parsley, chopped
1-1/2 oz. pkg. onion soup mix

2 c. water
1/4 t. dried oregano
1/4 t. dried basil
1/4 t. pepper
1 bay leaf
Garnish: grated Parmesan
   cheese

Combine all ingredients except cheese in a large Dutch oven.
Bring to a boil; reduce heat, cover and simmer for 30 minutes,
stirring occasionally. Add a little water if too thick. Add meatballs;
simmer an additional 20 to 30 minutes. Discard bay leaf. Sprinkle
with Parmesan cheese. Makes 6 servings.

Meatballs:

1-1/2 lbs. ground beef
1 egg, beaten
1/2 c. soft bread crumbs
1/4 c. grated Parmesan cheese
3 T. water

1 T. fresh parsley, chopped
1 t. garlic, minced
1/4 t. salt
2 T. butter, sliced

Combine all ingredients except butter; mix lightly and shape into
24 meatballs. Sauté in butter until browned on all sides; drain.

Plan-Over Instructions:
Triple meatball recipe to make 72 meatballs; divide into 3 portions
of 24 each. Reserve 2 portions for Italian Meatball Subs on page
81 and Good Ol' Spaghetti & Meatballs on page 82.

Italian Meatball Subs

Dana Thompson
Gooseberry Patch

Pass any leftover sauce for dipping.

1 onion, sliced
1/2 c. green pepper, chopped
2 T. water
8-oz. can pizza sauce
24 meatballs

4 Italian hard rolls, sliced
    and hollowed out
1/2 c. shredded provolone
    cheese

Combine onion, pepper and water in a large saucepan over medium heat. Cover and cook just until tender; drain. Stir in pizza sauce and meatballs; cook until hot and bubbly. Fill each roll with 6 meatballs; top with sauce mixture. Sprinkle with cheese and add tops. Place sandwiches in a lightly greased 13"x9" baking pan. Bake at 400 degrees for 10 to 15 minutes, until crusty and cheese is melted. Makes 4 servings.

Making a big batch of meatballs? Brown them the easy way...simply place meatballs in a roasting pan and bake for 15 to 20 minutes at 375 degrees.

Good Ol' Spaghetti & Meatballs

Diana Chaney
Olathe, KS

*Just the thing when Junior brings home friends from school...
easy to halve for a smaller group.*

2 14-1/2 oz. cans chunky
   diced tomatoes
2 6-oz. cans tomato paste
2/3 c. water
1 t. Italian seasoning

24 meatballs
16-oz. pkg. thin spaghetti,
   cooked
Garnish: grated Parmesan
   cheese

Combine tomatoes, tomato sauce, water and seasoning in a
medium saucepan. Bring to a boil over medium heat; reduce heat
and simmer for 5 minutes. Add meatballs and heat through. Ladle
sauce and meatballs over cooked spaghetti; sprinkle with cheese.
Makes 8 servings.

Extra cooked pasta doesn't need to go to waste. Toss with
oil, wrap tightly and refrigerate up to 4 days. To serve,
place in a metal colander, dip into boiling water for one
minute and drain...as good as fresh-cooked!

Once-a-Week Cooking

Freezer meals
to make ahead

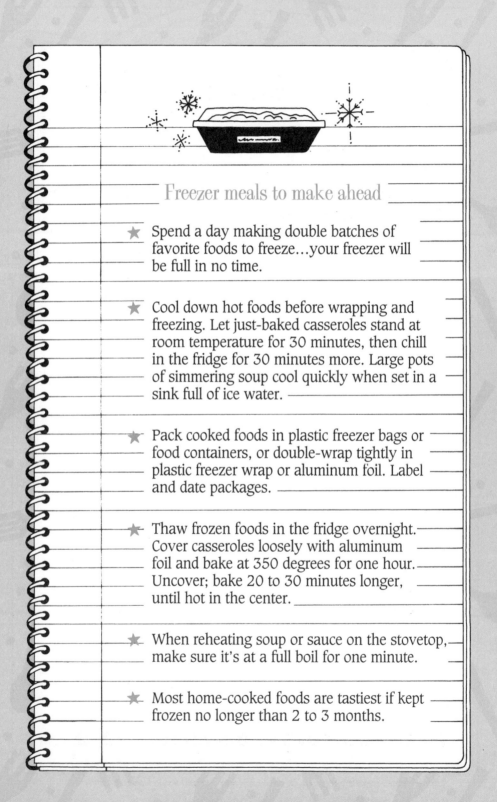

Freezer meals to make ahead

★ Spend a day making double batches of favorite foods to freeze...your freezer will be full in no time.

★ Cool down hot foods before wrapping and freezing. Let just-baked casseroles stand at room temperature for 30 minutes, then chill in the fridge for 30 minutes more. Large pots of simmering soup cool quickly when set in a sink full of ice water.

★ Pack cooked foods in plastic freezer bags or food containers, or double-wrap tightly in plastic freezer wrap or aluminum foil. Label and date packages.

★ Thaw frozen foods in the fridge overnight. Cover casseroles loosely with aluminum foil and bake at 350 degrees for one hour. Uncover; bake 20 to 30 minutes longer, until hot in the center.

★ When reheating soup or sauce on the stovetop, make sure it's at a full boil for one minute.

★ Most home-cooked foods are tastiest if kept frozen no longer than 2 to 3 months.

Spicy Fried Chicken

Lisa Allbright
Crockett, TX

Every day is a picnic when there's fried chicken for dinner.

2 c. all-purpose flour
1 T. salt
1/2 T. pepper
2 T. Cajun seasoning
1/2 T. garlic powder

1/2 T. onion powder
4 eggs, beaten
1/4 to 1/2 c. milk
6 lbs. chicken
oil for frying

Combine flour and seasonings in a large plastic zipping bag; set aside. Mix together eggs and milk. Shake chicken in flour mixture, then dip in egg mixture. Heat 1/4 inch oil in a large skillet over medium heat. Fry chicken until golden. Reduce heat and cook until juices run clear, turning several times, about 30 minutes. Serve immediately, or let cool, wrap in serving-size packages in aluminum foil and freeze for up to one month. Serves 6 to 8.

Heat & Eat Instructions:
Remove from freezer one hour before baking; thaw at room temperature. Open up wrapping and place package on oven rack. Bake at 375 degrees for 45 minutes, until heated through.

Brrr...don't let delicious frozen foods get freezer burn. Open the freezer door as little as possible to keep warm air out and fresh taste in.

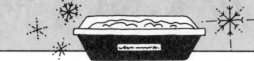

Beef & Bean Burritos

Nichole Martelli
Alvin, TX

The burritos are frozen individually...oh-so-handy for preparing just the number of servings you need.

1/4 c. oil
2 onions, chopped
4 lbs. ground beef
4 cloves garlic, minced
2 T. chili powder

2 t. ground cumin
salt and pepper to taste
16-oz. can tomato sauce
62-oz. can refried beans
24 10-inch flour tortillas

Heat oil in a large skillet over medium heat; cook onions until tender. Add ground beef and garlic; cook until browned. Drain; add seasonings and mix well. Stir in sauce; simmer for 5 minutes. Add beans; cook and stir until well blended. Cool slightly. Spread mixture down centers of tortillas; roll up burrito-style and arrange seam-side down on a greased baking sheet. Bake at 350 degrees for 20 minutes and serve immediately, or let cool and freeze on baking sheet. When frozen, wrap individually or in pairs and store in plastic zipping freezer bags. Makes 2 dozen.

Heat & Eat Instructions:

Thaw desired number of burritos. Reheat on a baking sheet at 350 degrees for 15 to 25 minutes.

Easy Cheesy Enchiladas

Julie Neathery
Oak Grove, LA

*Garnish with dollops of sour cream and a sprinkle of
sliced green onions just before serving.*

3 lbs. ground beef
2 1-1/4 oz. pkgs. taco
  seasoning mix
1 to 1-1/2 c. water
16-oz. can refried beans
2 pkgs. 10-inch flour tortillas
10-3/4 oz. can cream of
  mushroom soup

10-3/4 oz. can cream of
  chicken soup
2 10-oz. cans tomatoes
  with chiles
1-1/2 lbs. pasteurized process
  cheese spread, cubed

Brown ground beef in a large skillet over medium heat; drain.
Add seasoning mix and water; simmer for 5 minutes. Add beans;
cook for an additional 5 minutes. Spread mixture down center
of tortillas; roll up. Arrange seam-side down in 2 lightly greased
13"x9" baking pans; set aside. Combine remaining ingredients in a
medium saucepan. Cook over medium heat until cheese is melted;
spoon over enchiladas. Cover tightly with aluminum foil and
freeze, or bake at 350 degrees for 15 minutes, until bubbly.
Makes 2 pans; each pan serves 6 to 8.

Heat & Eat Instructions:
Thaw overnight in refrigerator. Remove aluminum foil and follow
baking instructions above, covering again if top begins to brown.

Start a cooking club with friends!
Decide on dishes ahead of time,
then everyone shops for
just a part of the meal. Get
together to cook and pack
dishes in freezer containers.

Sausage Tortilla Roll-Ups

Becky Riedesel
Sioux City, IA

My aunt demonstrated this recipe on a local TV cooking show many years ago. It's easily doubled to make 2 pans... one to bake and one to freeze for later.

1-1/2 lbs. Italian ground pork sausage, browned and drained
2 c. cottage cheese
2 T. all-purpose flour
3 c. spaghetti sauce

1 t. dried basil
1 t. dried oregano
1/4 t. garlic powder
10 10-inch flour tortillas
1-1/2 c. shredded mozzarella cheese

Stir together sausage, cottage cheese and flour; set aside. Stir together sauce and seasonings; stir 1/2 cup sauce mixture into sausage mixture. Spoon 1/3 cup sausage mixture onto centers of tortillas; roll up and place seam-side down in a lightly greased 13"x9" baking pan. Pour remaining sauce mixture over tortillas. Cover tightly with aluminum foil and freeze, or bake, covered, at 375 degrees for 45 to 50 minutes, until bubbly. Uncover, sprinkle with cheese and return to oven for 3 to 5 minutes, or until cheese is melted. Serves 4 to 6.

Heat & Eat Instructions:
Thaw overnight in refrigerator. Follow baking instructions above, adding cheese as directed.

Don't tie up your favorite casserole dish in the freezer. Line it with aluminum foil, bake a casserole, wrap and freeze...lift out the frozen casserole and return the dish to the cupboard. To serve, slip the casserole back into the same dish and bake.

Broccoli Chicken & Rice

Heather Bartlett
Panama City, FL

A different kind of make-ahead meal that goes together quickly, then cooks up fresh at serving time.

2 c. cooked chicken, chopped
10-oz. pkg. frozen broccoli, thawed
1 c. carrot, peeled and sliced
1/2 c. onion, chopped
3 T. lemon juice
2 T. margarine
1 T. cornstarch

2 cubes chicken bouillon
4 t. dried parsley
1 t. lemon zest
1/2 t. salt
1/2 t. garlic, minced
1 c. long-cooking rice, uncooked
2 c. water

Combine all ingredients except rice and water; mix well. Spoon into a freezer-safe container and freeze, or spoon into a large saucepan. Bring to a boil over medium heat; add rice and water. Simmer, covered, over low heat for 20 minutes, or until rice is tender. Serves 4.

Heat & Eat Instructions:

Thaw overnight in refrigerator. Spoon into a large saucepan; follow cooking instructions above, adding rice and water as directed.

Cook up a big pot of chicken to freeze for later.
For juicy, flavorful chicken, cover with water and
simmer gently just until tender, then turn off the
heat and let the chicken cool in its own broth.

Creamy Mushroom Sauce

Jo Ann

*With this delicious sauce tucked in the freezer,
you can quickly make the chicken recipe on page 91...
try it for beef stroganoff too.*

1/3 c. oil
1/4 c. all-purpose flour
3 T. butter
6 c. sliced mushrooms
3/4 c. onion, finely chopped
3/4 t. dried thyme

1/2 t. salt
1/2 t. pepper
3 c. beef broth
1/3 c. cornstarch
3 c. milk

Combine oil, flour and butter in a large Dutch oven; cook and
stir over medium heat until golden. Stir in mushrooms, onion
and seasonings; cook until onion is tender. Combine broth and
cornstarch; add to mushroom mixture, stirring well. Add milk;
stir and cook over low heat until thickened and bubbly. Cook
for 2 additional minutes. Use immediately as desired or let cool,
divide into 3 plastic zipping freezer bags in 2-2/3 cup portions
and freeze. Makes about 8 cups sauce.

Heat & Eat Instructions:
Thaw overnight in refrigerator. Spoon into a microwave-safe bowl.
Microwave on medium-low setting, for 8 to 12 minutes, until hot,
stirring once.

A wide-mouth funnel is handy for filling freezer bags.
Stand the open bag in a bowl and hold the bag's
top closed around the bottom of the funnel,
then just ladle in soup or sauce.

Chicken & Mushroom Linguine   *Jo Ann*

Tastes like you cooked for hours!

8-oz. pkg. linguine pasta,
   uncooked
2 c. broccoli flowerets
2-2/3 c. Creamy Mushroom
   Sauce, thawed

2 T. dry sherry or beef broth
1 c. cooked chicken, cubed

Cook pasta according to package directions, adding broccoli
during last 4 minutes of cooking. Drain; cover and keep warm. In
a saucepan, bring Creamy Mushroom Sauce to a boil over medium
heat. Add sherry or broth; whisk until sauce is smooth. Stir in
chicken; heat through. Serve over hot pasta and broccoli mixture.
Serves 4.

Use square plastic freezer containers...they take up
less room in your freezer than round ones. To squeeze
in even more, ladle prepared food into plastic zipping bags,
seal and press flat. When frozen, they'll stack easily.

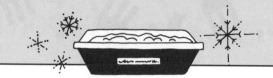

King Ranch Chicken Casserole

Linda Behling
Cecil, PA

Make a double batch...you'll be ready for the next school potluck!

1 c. onion, diced
1 c. green pepper, diced
8-oz. pkg. sliced mushrooms
1/4 c. butter
10-3/4 oz. can cream of
    mushroom soup
10-3/4 oz. can cream of
    chicken soup
10-oz. can tomatoes with chiles

1 clove garlic, minced
2 T. chili powder
1 T. chicken broth
2 c. cooked chicken, diced
12 6-inch corn tortillas, torn
    into quarters
16-oz. pkg. shredded Cheddar
    cheese

In a large skillet over medium heat, sauté onion, pepper and mushrooms in butter. Add soups, tomatoes, garlic, chili powder and broth; heat until bubbly and set aside. Arrange half the tortillas in a lightly greased 13"x9" baking pan; top with half the chicken, half the sauce and half the cheese. Repeat layers. Cover tightly with aluminum foil and freeze, or bake at 350 degrees for about 30 minutes, until hot and bubbly. Serves 6.

Heat & Eat Instructions:
Thaw overnight in refrigerator. Follow baking instructions above.

It's best not to add sour cream or mayonnaise to dishes that will be frozen...they tend to separate. Instead, stir these ingredients into thawed food just before reheating.

Honey-Pepper Pork

Gloria Warren
Corbeil, Ontario

This has become one of my favorite recipes. It's great over rice.

1-1/2 lbs. boneless pork loin,
   cubed
2 T. oil
.75-oz. pkg. brown gravy mix
1 c. water
1/4 c. honey
3 T. soy sauce

2 T. red wine vinegar
1/2 t. ground ginger
1/8 t. garlic powder
1 green pepper, chopped
1 red pepper, chopped
1 onion, chopped

In a large skillet over medium heat, sauté pork in oil until browned, about 15 minutes. Add gravy mix, water, honey, soy sauce, vinegar, ginger and garlic powder; stir well. Cover and reduce heat to low; simmer for 15 minutes, until sauce thickens. Add peppers and onion; let cool, package in a plastic zipping freezer bag and freeze, or simmer until vegetables are tender. Serves 4.

Heat & Eat Instructions:
Thaw overnight in refrigerator. Pour into a saucepan; cover and simmer over medium heat until heated through and vegetables are tender.

On a leisurely day,
bake up a double batch
of cookies and freeze them.
Later, your family can
enjoy home-baked goodies
even at busy times...
simply thaw and serve!

Saucy Meatloaf

Gloria Schantz
Breinigsville, PA

Real old-fashioned comfort food...serve with mashed potatoes.

1-1/2 lbs. ground beef
1 egg, beaten
1 c. fresh bread crumbs
1/2 c. milk

3 T. red steak sauce
1-1/4 t. salt
1/8 t. pepper
Garnish: additional steak sauce

Combine all ingredients thoroughly; place in a lightly greased
9"x5" loaf pan. Turn out of pan, wrap well and freeze, or bake at
350 degrees for one hour, brushing top with additional sauce.
Let meatloaf stand for 5 minutes before slicing. Serves 6 to 8.

Heat & Eat Instructions:
Unwrap meatloaf; place in loaf pan as above, cover and thaw
overnight in refrigerator. Follow baking instructions above.

Bake up some mini meatloaves for smaller appetites...fill
muffin tins and freeze. Pop them out and place in a
freezer bag. Just heat up what you need.

Easy Veggie Beef Soup

Christina Mamula
Aliquippa, PA

*Another easy way to cook up this soup…
combine all the ingredients in a slow cooker, cover
and cook on low setting for 7 to 8 hours.*

1 lb. stew beef, cubed
4 potatoes, peeled and cubed
2 stalks celery, sliced
46-oz. can cocktail vegetable
   juice
3 10-1/2 oz. cans beef
   consommé

2 14-1/2 oz. cans diced
   tomatoes
24-oz. pkg. frozen green beans
16-oz. pkg. frozen corn
16-oz. pkg. frozen peas
8-oz. pkg. frozen sliced carrots
salt and pepper to taste

Combine all ingredients in a large soup pot; add enough water to cover. Bring to a boil over medium heat. Reduce heat, cover and simmer for about one hour, until meat and potatoes are tender. Serve immediately, or cool, ladle into freezer-safe containers and freeze. Serves 6 to 8.

Heat & Eat Instructions:
Thaw overnight in refrigerator. Pour into a saucepan; heat over medium heat until hot and bubbly.

Slow cookers are oh-so-handy for cooking up big batches to freeze! No stirring, no sticking and they don't heat up the kitchen. You may even want to borrow an extra one for a big cooking day.

All-Purpose Ground Beef Mix

Nichole Martelli
Alvin, TX

*Speed up recipes like stuffed peppers and spaghetti sauce
with this seasoned meat mix tucked into the freezer.*

5 lbs. ground beef
4 stalks celery, diced
1 clove garlic, minced

2 onions, diced
1 green pepper, diced
salt and pepper to taste

Brown ground beef in a large skillet over medium heat; drain. Stir
in celery, garlic, onions and pepper; add salt and pepper to taste.
Cover skillet; simmer until vegetables are tender, about 15 to
20 minutes. Let cool. Divide into recipe-size portions in plastic
zipping freezer bags; freeze. Makes about 12 cups of meat mix.

Heat & Eat Instructions:

Thaw desired amount in refrigerator overnight. Use in recipes
calling for browned ground beef, like Aaron's Favorite Chili
on the next page.

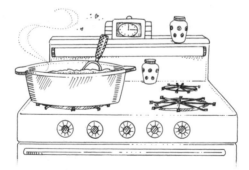

A nothing-to-it way to brown lots of ground beef at once...
simply put it in a large roasting pan. Bake at 350 degrees
until browned, chopping occasionally with a potato masher
as it browns. So much easier than standing over the stove!

Aaron's Favorite Chili

Nichole Martelli
Alvin, TX

My husband just can't get enough of this spicy chili!

4 c. All-Purpose Ground Beef
   Mix, thawed
3 16-oz. cans corn, drained
2 32-oz. cans crushed
   tomatoes

4 16-oz. cans kidney beans,
   drained and rinsed
2 T. chili powder
2 T. ground cumin

Combine all ingredients in a large stockpot over medium heat.
Bring to a boil; reduce heat and simmer for one hour, stirring
occasionally. Serve immediately or let cool, ladle into freezer-safe
containers and freeze. Makes 12 to 15 servings.

Heat & Eat Instructions:

Thaw overnight in refrigerator. Pour into a saucepan; heat over
medium heat until hot and bubbly.

Contents: _____
Serves: _____
Prepared on: _____
Enjoy by: _____
Cooking Instructions: _____
_____
_____
_____
_____

Copy & cut this handy label to ensure freezer-fresh foods!

Granny's Chicken Spaghetti

Megan Brooks
Antioch, TN

For a smaller family, divide the chicken mixture into 2 freezer packages. Combine each with an 8-ounce package of spaghetti.

1 onion, chopped
1 green pepper, chopped
2 T. oil
4 boneless, skinless chicken
    breasts, cooked and cubed
10-3/4 oz. can cream of
    mushroom soup

1-1/2 c. sour cream
16-oz. pkg. pasteurized
    process cheese spread
8-oz. can sliced water
    chestnuts, drained
7-oz. jar pimentos, drained
16-oz. pkg. spaghetti, cooked

In a large skillet over medium heat, sauté onion and pepper in oil until tender. Add remaining ingredients except spaghetti; mix well and simmer until cheese is melted. Spread spaghetti in a greased deep 13"x9" baking pan. Top with chicken mixture. Bake at 350 degrees for 45 minutes, or until heated through. Or cool chicken mixture, package in a plastic zipping freezer bag and freeze for later use. Serves 6 to 8.

Heat & Eat Instructions:

Thaw overnight in refrigerator. Follow baking instructions above, combining with freshly cooked spaghetti as directed.

Crumb toppings for frozen casseroles will be crispy and crunchy if they're added just before reheating.

Italian Sausage Lasagna

Francie Stutzman
Dalton, OH

This lasagna tastes wonderful and it freezes well too.

1 lb. mild Italian ground pork
    sausage, browned and
    drained
16-oz. can diced tomatoes
2 6-oz. cans tomato paste
1 clove garlic, minced
1 T. dried basil
1 T. dried parsley

3-1/2 t. salt, divided
3 c. cottage cheese
2 eggs, beaten
1/2 c. grated Parmesan cheese
1/2 t. pepper
10-oz. pkg. lasagna, cooked
16-oz. pkg. shredded
    mozzarella cheese

In a skillet over medium heat, combine sausage, tomatoes, tomato paste, garlic, herbs and 1-1/2 teaspoons salt. Simmer for 45 minutes, stirring occasionally. Combine cottage cheese, eggs, Parmesan cheese, remaining salt and pepper; set aside. Arrange half of lasagna strips in a lightly greased 13"x9" baking pan, followed by half each of meat mixture, cottage cheese mixture and mozzarella cheese. Repeat layers, ending with mozzarella. Bake, uncovered, at 375 degrees for 30 minutes. Remove from oven; let stand 15 minutes. If freezing, cool completely before wrapping. Makes 6 to 8 servings.

Heat & Eat Instructions:

Thaw overnight in refrigerator. Bake, uncovered, at 375 degrees for 45 minutes, or until hot and bubbly.

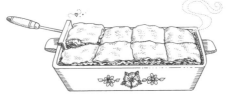

Cut baked lasagna into serving portions and freeze on a baking sheet, then pack frozen portions in a freezer bag. Later you'll be able to heat up just the number of servings you need.

Hungarian Goulash

Bev Westfall
Berlin, NY

*A hearty dish that's a long-time favorite of my family.
Add some green pepper along with the ground beef or
spice it up with garlic, fresh parsley or oregano.*

3/4 lb. ground beef
2 T. onion, chopped
1 c. elbow macaroni, cooked
1 c. shredded mozzarella cheese

10-3/4 oz. can tomato soup
1/2 c. Italian-seasoned dry
   bread crumbs
2 T. butter, diced

Brown ground beef and onion in a large skillet over medium heat; drain. Layer half each of macaroni, meat mixture, cheese and soup in a lightly greased 2-1/2 quart casserole dish. Repeat layers; top with bread crumbs and dot with butter. Cover tightly with aluminum foil and freeze, or bake at 350 degrees for one hour. Serves 4.

Heat & Eat Instructions:
Thaw overnight in refrigerator. Follow baking instructions above.

Freeze uncooked chicken, beef or pork cutlets with marinade in freezer bags. After thawing overnight in the fridge, meat can go right to the skillet or grill for a delicious meal.

Freezer Taco Rice

Patricia Wissler
Harrisburg, PA

Yummy! Add your favorite toppings like shredded cheese and sour cream to make taco salad or roll up burritos in a jiffy.

3 lbs. ground beef, turkey or
   chicken
3 c. onion, diced
3 1-1/4 oz. pkgs. taco
   seasoning mix

6 c. cooked white or brown rice
3 16-oz. cans diced tomatoes
2 8-oz. pkgs. shredded
   Mexican-blend cheese

Brown meat in a large saucepan over medium heat; drain. Add onion, taco seasoning, rice and tomatoes; simmer until thickened, about 30 minutes. Stir in cheese; cool completely. Package in 3 freezer-safe containers; freeze. Makes 3 containers; each container serves 4 to 6.

Heat & Eat Instructions:
Thaw overnight in refrigerator. Reheat in a saucepan over medium heat and use as desired.

Oops, the family's dinner plans have changed, and dinner is already thawing. No problem! As long as some ice crystals remain, it's perfectly safe to return partially defrosted food to the freezer.

James' Sloppy Joes

Lisa Allbright
Crockett, TX

Toast the buns first...no more sogginess!

2 lbs. ground beef
1 onion, chopped
1/2 c. green pepper, chopped
1/2 c. celery, chopped
2 14-1/2 oz. cans stewed
   tomatoes
2 c. tomato sauce

1/2 c. catsup
1/4 c. brown sugar, packed
2 T. spicy mustard
1 T. Worcestershire sauce
1/4 t. salt
1/4 t. pepper
6 to 8 sandwich buns, split

Brown ground beef, onion, green pepper and celery in a large skillet over medium heat; drain. Add remaining ingredients except buns. Bring to a boil; reduce heat and simmer for one hour, stirring occasionally. Spoon onto buns and serve, or cool completely and package in freezer-safe containers. Serves 6 to 8.

Heat & Eat Instructions:
Thaw overnight in refrigerator. In a saucepan, reheat over medium heat until hot and bubbly. Serve on buns.

Turn leftover Sloppy Joe sauce into a tasty quick casserole... spread it in a baking pan, top with refrigerated biscuits and cheese slices. Bake until bubbly and biscuits are golden.

Cheesy Chicken Bake

Pam James
Gooseberry Patch

It's not necessary to thaw the frozen veggies if you're preparing this casserole to go straight into the freezer.

10-3/4 oz. can cream of
   chicken soup
1 c. sour cream
1/4 c. milk
2 c. cooked chicken, cubed
2-1/2 c. shredded Cheddar
   cheese, divided

3-1/2 c. frozen shredded
   hashbrowns, thawed
1-1/2 c. frozen peppers and
   onions, thawed
1-1/2 c. potato chips, crushed

Combine soup, sour cream, milk, chicken and 1-1/4 cups cheese in a large bowl. Spread 3/4 of mixture in a greased 2-quart casserole dish. Sprinkle hashbrowns, peppers and onions over top, pressing down lightly. Top with remaining soup mixture and cheese. Wrap casserole and freeze, or sprinkle with chips and bake, uncovered, at 350 degrees for 50 to 60 minutes, until bubbly. Let stand for 5 to 10 minutes before serving. Serves 8.

Heat & Eat Instructions:

Thaw overnight in refrigerator. Uncover and bake at 350 degrees for 60 to 70 minutes, until bubbly. Top with chips and bake for a few minutes longer.

Get out Grandma's oversized mixing bowl...it's just the thing for stirring up double and triple batches.

Mexican Meat Mix

Terri Steffes
Jefferson City, MO

Another versatile ground beef mix to keep on hand.

4 lbs. ground beef
1 onion, finely chopped
3 c. tomato sauce
3 T. ground cumin

3 cloves garlic, chopped
salt and pepper to taste
1/2 c. fresh Italian parsley,
   chopped

Brown ground beef and onion in a large skillet over medium heat.
Drain; add tomato sauce, cumin, garlic, salt and pepper. Stir in
parsley; cook until thickened. Cool completely; package in one-cup
portions in freezer-safe containers. Makes 10 cups.

Heat & Eat Instructions:

Thaw desired amount in refrigerator overnight. Use in recipes
calling for browned ground beef with tomato sauce, like
Tex-Mex Stuffed Peppers on the next page.

Prevent tomato sauce from staining white plastic
freezer containers...easy! Just spray the container
with non-stick vegetable spray before filling.

Tex-Mex Stuffed Peppers

Terri Steffes
Jefferson City, MO

*No leftover Spanish rice on hand? Just stir
some salsa into plain white cooked rice.*

2 T. olive oil, divided
4 poblano peppers, halved
   and seeded
4 c. baby spinach
1 clove garlic, pressed
salt and pepper

2 c. Mexican Meat Mix, thawed
1 c. cooked Spanish rice
8-oz. can tomato sauce
8-oz. pkg. shredded Monterey
   Jack cheese

Heat one tablespoon oil in a large skillet over medium heat; sauté
pepper halves until softened. Remove peppers; set aside. Heat
remaining oil in skillet; sauté spinach, garlic, salt and pepper
until wilted. Spoon spinach mixture into pepper halves; wrap and
freeze, or place on a broiler pan and set aside. Combine meat mix,
rice and tomato sauce in skillet; heat through. Spoon meat mixture
over peppers; sprinkle with cheese and place under a broiler just
until cheese melts. Makes 4 servings.

Heat & Eat Instructions:

Thaw peppers and meat mix overnight in refrigerator. Add rice and
sauce to meat mix as directed above. In a microwave-safe dish,
top peppers with meat mixture and cheese. Microwave on high
setting until heated through.

Post a list of freezer meals right on the fridge and
cross them off as they're served. You'll always know
what's on the menu for tonight.

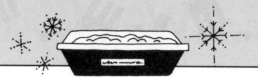

Family-Friendly Spaghetti

Ellen Stringer
Bourbonnais, IL

This recipe won an honorable mention when I entered it in a local newspaper's recipe contest. Kids love it! I've made many batches to share with new moms and their families.

11 c. water
16-oz. pkg. spaghetti, uncooked
1-1/2 oz. pkg. onion soup mix
.75-oz. pkg. garlic & herb soup mix
1 lb. Italian ground pork sausage

1 lb. ground beef
2 8-oz. cans tomato sauce
2 6-oz. cans tomato paste
2 T. dried parsley
2 t. dried Italian seasoning
2 t. garlic powder

Bring water to a boil in a large stockpot over medium-high heat; add spaghetti and soup mixes. Cook for 8 to 10 minutes, stirring occasionally, until spaghetti is tender; do not drain. Set aside. Brown sausage and ground beef in a large saucepan; drain. Add remaining ingredients; mix well. Add meat mixture to spaghetti mixture, stirring well. Simmer over low heat to desired consistency, 20 to 30 minutes. Serve immediately or let cool, spoon into freezer-safe containers and freeze. Serves 10 to 12.

Heat & Eat Instructions:
Thaw overnight in refrigerator. Pour into a saucepan; simmer over low heat until heated through.

When making a double batch of a recipe, add just 1-1/2 times the herbs and seasoning. Taste and add more if needed.

Carolyn's Chicken Tetrazzini

Carolyn Knight
Oklahoma City, OK

Scrumptious made with leftover holiday turkey too.

2 c. sliced mushrooms
1/4 c. butter
3 T. all-purpose flour
2 c. chicken broth
1/4 c. light cream
3 T. sherry or chicken broth
1 T. fresh parsley, chopped

1 t. salt
1/8 t. pepper
1/8 t. nutmeg
3 c. cooked chicken, cubed
8-oz. pkg. spaghetti, cooked
1 c. grated Parmesan cheese

In a Dutch oven over medium heat, sauté mushrooms in butter until tender. Stir in flour. Add chicken broth; cook, stirring constantly until sauce is thickened. Remove from heat; stir in cream, sherry or broth and seasonings. Fold in chicken and cooked spaghetti; turn mixture into a lightly greased 13"x9" baking pan. Sprinkle with Parmesan cheese. Cool; cover with aluminum foil and freeze, or bake at 350 degrees for 30 to 35 minutes, until heated through. Let stand for 5 to 10 minutes. Serves 8.

Heat & Eat Instructions:
Thaw overnight in refrigerator. Uncover and follow baking instructions above.

The discovery of a new dish does more for human happiness than the discovery of a new star.

-Anthelme Brillat-Savarin

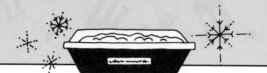

Polynesian Spareribs

Molly Cool
Gooseberry Patch

*Double the recipe and freeze...
you'll be ready for the next game day!*

4 lbs. pork spareribs, cut into
   serving-size portions
2 onions, chopped
2 carrots, peeled and chopped
2 T. oil
1-1/3 c. pineapple juice
2/3 c. red wine vinegar

2 T. Worcestershire sauce
2 t. soy sauce
2/3 c. brown sugar, packed
2 T. cornstarch
1/2 c. water
juice and zest of 1 lemon
salt and pepper to taste

Arrange spareribs in a large roasting pan; bake at 425 degrees
for 20 minutes. Drain drippings from pan; set ribs aside. In a
saucepan over medium heat, sauté vegetables in oil until tender.
Add pineapple juice, vinegar, sauces and sugar, stirring until
sugar dissolves. Simmer over low heat for 20 minutes, stirring
occasionally. Combine cornstarch and water in a small bowl; stir
into sauce along with lemon juice, zest, salt and pepper. Bring
to a boil, stirring constantly. Reduce heat to low; simmer for
2 to 3 minutes, until thickened. Pour sauce over ribs. Bake
at 350 degrees for 40 minutes, basting every 10 minutes.
Serve hot, or let cool, wrap in aluminum foil and freeze.
Makes 4 to 6 servings.

Heat & Eat Instructions:
Thaw overnight in refrigerator. Place in roasting pan; cover. Bake
at 400 degrees for 30 minutes; uncover and bake an additional
15 minutes.

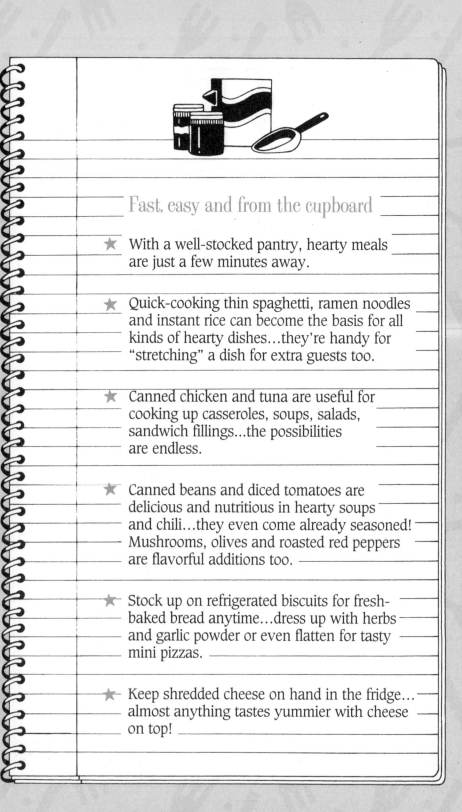

Fast, easy and from the cupboard

★ With a well-stocked pantry, hearty meals are just a few minutes away.

★ Quick-cooking thin spaghetti, ramen noodles and instant rice can become the basis for all kinds of hearty dishes...they're handy for "stretching" a dish for extra guests too.

★ Canned chicken and tuna are useful for cooking up casseroles, soups, salads, sandwich fillings...the possibilities are endless.

★ Canned beans and diced tomatoes are delicious and nutritious in hearty soups and chili...they even come already seasoned! Mushrooms, olives and roasted red peppers are flavorful additions too.

★ Stock up on refrigerated biscuits for fresh-baked bread anytime...dress up with herbs and garlic powder or even flatten for tasty mini pizzas.

★ Keep shredded cheese on hand in the fridge... almost anything tastes yummier with cheese on top!

Homestyle Chicken & Rice

Teresa Powers
Watkinsville, GA

*This easy-to-fix dish goes over very well with my family...
and canned chicken is a real time-saver for me.*

10-1/2 oz. can chicken broth
10-3/4 oz. can cream of chicken
   soup
2 10-oz. cans chicken, drained
1 onion, diced

1/2 c. butter
salt and pepper to taste
1 c. instant rice, uncooked
Garnish: crushed potato chips
   or crispy rice cereal

Heat together broth and soup in a saucepan over medium heat.
Add chicken, onion, butter, salt and pepper to taste. Simmer over
low heat for about 5 minutes; add rice and stir well. Pour into a
greased 13"x9" baking pan; top with potato chips or cereal. Bake
at 350 degrees for 30 minutes. Serves 4.

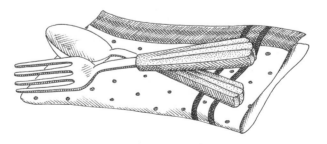

A Lazy Susan is oh-so handy for keeping cans and
bottles at your fingertips...bring the item you need to
the front of the cupboard with just a spin of the base!

Creamed Chicken & Biscuits

Kathy Grashoff
Fort Wayne, IN

Mmm...real comfort food.

2 c. cooked chicken, diced
10-oz. pkg. frozen mixed
   vegetables
10-3/4 oz. can cream of
   chicken soup
1/2 c. milk

1/2 t. poultry seasoning
1/4 t. pepper
6-oz. tube refrigerated
   buttermilk biscuits,
   baked and split

Combine all ingredients except biscuits in a medium saucepan. Simmer over medium heat for 10 to 15 minutes, until heated through and vegetables are tender. To serve, spoon over split biscuit halves. Serves 4.

Buy ready-to-eat meat at the supermarket deli counter for quick pantry meals. Just order what you need, have it sliced thick, then cube or dice to use in recipes.

Pantry Meals

Pork Chops Olé

Linda Davidson
Lexington, KY

*Try this with Mexican-blend shredded cheese if
your family likes extra-spicy foods.*

2 T. olive oil
6 pork chops, cut 1/2-inch thick
seasoned salt and pepper
   to taste
3/4 c. long-cooking rice,
   uncooked

1-1/2 c. water
8-oz. can tomato sauce
2 T. taco seasoning mix
1 green pepper, chopped
1 c. shredded Cheddar cheese

Heat oil in a large skillet over medium heat; add pork chops and
brown on both sides. Sprinkle with salt and pepper; set aside.
Combine rice, water, tomato sauce and taco seasoning; mix well.
Pour into a lightly greased 13"x9" baking pan; arrange pork on top
of rice mixture. Sprinkle with green pepper; cover and bake at
350 degrees for 30 to 45 minutes. Uncover; sprinkle with cheese.
Return to oven and bake until cheese melts. Serves 4 to 6.

Keep a permanent marker handy in the kitchen to
write the purchase date on food cans and boxes...
you'll always know how fresh they are.

Tex-Mex Tortilla Soup

Trisha Fipps
Dunbar, WI

*I like to serve this easy-to-make soup with
homemade quesadillas...delicious.*

3 10-3/4 oz. cans chicken &
   rice soup
2 10-oz. can tomatoes with
   chiles
15-1/4 oz. can corn, drained

8-oz. can tomato sauce
2 to 3 c. tortilla chips, crushed
8-oz. pkg. shredded Monterey
   Jack cheese

Combine soup, tomatoes, corn and tomato sauce in a large pot;
simmer over medium heat until heated through. To serve, place a
handful of crushed tortilla chips and 1/4 cup cheese in bottom of
each bowl. Ladle soup over top. Serves 4 to 6.

Give any chunky soup a creamier texture without adding
cream. Spoon out some of the cooked vegetables and purée
in a blender, then stir back into the soup and heat through.

Pantry Meals

Mom's Vegetable Soup

Lauren Williams
Kewanee, MO

My family's favorite comfort food...my mother always made it when the weather turned cold or rainy. It's scrumptious served with cornbread crumbled in the soup bowl.

16-oz. pkg. frozen garden
   vegetable blend
1 onion, chopped
4 potatoes, peeled and diced

46-oz. can tomato juice
3 c. water
1 T. oil
1 t. salt

Combine all ingredients in a large soup pot. Bring to a boil over medium heat; boil for 20 minutes. Reduce heat and simmer for one hour. Soup will thicken as it simmers. Makes 4 to 6 servings.

There's nothing cozier than grilled cheese and soup for supper!
Just for fun, make grilled cheese sandwiches in a waffle iron.

Yummy Beef Bake

Sharon Tillman
Hampton, VA

A tasty stick-to-your-ribs dish...oh-so-easy.

1 lb. ground beef, browned
   and drained
10-3/4 oz. can cream of
   chicken soup

1 c. sour cream
12-oz. pkg. medium egg
   noodles, cooked

Combine ground beef, soup and sour cream in a skillet; bring
to a simmer and set aside. Place cooked noodles in a greased
1-1/2 quart casserole dish; pour beef mixture evenly over top.
Bake at 350 degrees for 30 minutes, until hot and bubbly.
Serves 4.

Keep a kitchen journal...jot down favorite recipes and family
members' preferences. It'll make meal planning a snap!

Pantry Meals

1-2-3 Chili Enchiladas

Becky Christie
Columbia, MD

Toss together a crisp salad of shredded lettuce, sliced tomato and avocado...dinner is ready!

2 15-oz. cans chili without beans
6 8-inch flour tortillas

8-oz. pkg. shredded Cheddar cheese, divided

Pour one can of chili into a microwave-safe bowl; heat on high setting for 45 seconds. Spoon hot chili down centers of tortillas; sprinkle half the cheese over top of chili. Roll tortillas up and place seam-side down in a lightly greased 13"x9" baking pan. Pour remaining chili over top of enchiladas; sprinkle with remaining cheese. Bake at 350 degrees for 20 minutes, or until heated through. Serves 6.

Keep canned beans on hand for quick & tasty pantry meals like chili, cold salads and hot side dishes. With lots of kinds to choose from like Great Northern, red kidney, white cannellini and black turtle beans, meals are never boring!

Denise's Garlic Fettuccine

Denise Mainville
Huber Heights, OH

Simple and filling.

4 cloves garlic, minced
1/2 c. olive oil
1 t. salt
1/2 t. Italian seasoning
1/4 c. butter

1/2 c. hot water
16-oz. pkg. fettuccine pasta,
   cooked
Garnish: grated Parmesan
   cheese

Sauté garlic with oil in a skillet over medium heat. Stir in salt and Italian seasoning; set aside. Melt butter in hot water and add to garlic mixture; stir to mix well. Add garlic mixture to pasta and toss to blend. Garnish with Parmesan cheese. Serves 4.

Use a potato peeler to quickly cut thin curls of
cheese for garnishing pasta, soup or salads.

Pantry Meals

Ham & Linguine Toss

Melinda Grunden
Cecil, OH

This is a good summer meal, since it goes together quickly and doesn't heat up the kitchen. The leftovers are even good cold.

16-oz. pkg. linguine pasta, uncooked
2 c. frozen peas, thawed
1/2 c. margarine

2 c. cooked ham, cubed
1/2 to 1 c. grated Parmesan cheese

Cook pasta according to package instructions, adding peas during the last 3 minutes of cooking. Drain and return to pan; add margarine and stir until melted. Add ham and Parmesan cheese; mix well and briefly heat through. Serves 6.

Frozen veggies come in so many delicious mixtures...
and they're almost as good as homegrown.
Add variety to favorite recipes or toss with
dried herbs and crispy bacon for a quick side.

Cheeseburger & Fries Casserole

*Judy Lange
Imperial, PA*

Kids love it!

2 lbs. ground beef, browned and drained
10-3/4 oz. can golden mushroom soup
10-3/4 oz. Cheddar cheese soup
20-oz. pkg. frozen crinkle-cut French fries

Combine ground beef and soups; mix well and pour into a lightly greased 13"x9" baking pan. Arrange French fries on top. Bake, uncovered, at 350 degrees for 50 to 55 minutes, until fries are golden. Serves 6 to 8.

A casserole that's baked uncovered will have a crisper, more golden topping than one that's covered during baking...it's your choice.

Quick Pizza Mac

Sheila Murray
Lancaster, CA

*Another kid-friendly recipe...tasty fixed with sliced
hot dogs instead of pepperoni too.*

1-1/2 c. elbow macaroni, cooked
8-oz. jar pizza sauce
8-oz. container cottage cheese
4-oz. pkg. sliced pepperoni,
  halved

1/2 c. onion, chopped
1/2 t. dried basil
1 T. grated Parmesan cheese

In a lightly greased 2-quart casserole dish, combine all ingredients
except Parmesan cheese; blend well. Sprinkle Parmesan over top.
Cover; bake at 350 degrees for 30 to 35 minutes, or until heated
through. Serves 6.

No muss, no fuss...toss salad fixings and dressing in a
plastic zipping bag, spoon out the salad, then toss the bag!

Camp Kettle Stew

Kerry Woodham
Dothan, AL

Once you've opened all the cans, dinner is almost ready!

2 14-1/2 oz. cans diced
   tomatoes
10-oz. can tomatoes with chiles
2 10-oz. cans chicken, drained
2 15-oz. cans corn, drained
15-oz. can lima beans, drained
   and rinsed
15-oz. can peas, drained
15-oz. can green beans,
   drained
15-oz. can sliced carrots,
   drained
1/2 c. barbecue sauce
2 T. Worcestershire sauce
3-3/4 c. water
hot pepper sauce to taste

Combine all ingredients in a large saucepan; bring to a boil over medium heat. Reduce heat and simmer for 10 minutes. Makes 18 to 20 servings.

Have a picnic indoors. Spread blankets on the floor in front of the fireplace and serve big bowls of Camp Kettle Stew. Afterwards, toast marshmallows for dessert. What fun!

Cheesy Ham & Broccoli Soup

Heather Torrence
Rothsay, MN

Wonderful on a chilly day.

3 10-3/4 oz. cans Cheddar
   cheese soup
2-1/2 c. milk
1-1/4 c. water
2 c. cooked ham, cubed

10-oz. pkg. frozen chopped
   broccoli
14-1/2 oz. can sliced potatoes,
   drained
1/2 onion, chopped

Whisk together soups, milk and water until creamy. Combine
with remaining ingredients in a large soup pot. Simmer over
medium-low heat for 45 minutes, until broccoli and onion are
tender. Serves 4 to 6.

Talk of joy: there may be things better than beef stew and
baked potatoes and homemade bread...there may be.

-David Grayson

Baked Pancake Chicken

Angela Farrell
Boise, ID

A traditional Czech dish, delicious with country gravy.

6 boneless, skinless chicken
    breasts, cooked and cubed
1/4 c. olive oil
3 eggs, beaten

1/8 t. salt
1 c. milk
1 to 1-1/2 c. all-purpose flour

Arrange chicken in a lightly greased 13"x9" baking pan; set aside.
Mix together remaining ingredients, adding enough flour to make
a consistency a little thinner than pancake batter. Pour over
chicken. Bake at 375 degrees for 25 minutes, or until golden.
Cut into squares to serve. Serves 4 to 6.

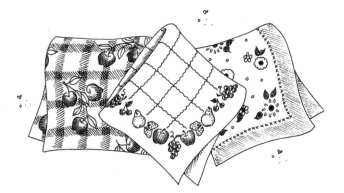

Stir cinnamon into apple pie filling and simmer gently
until hot and bubbly, for a simple side dish
that's especially good with pork.

Pantry Meals

Sweet-and-Sour Chicken

Pam Hood
Pipersville, PA

Can't find Russian salad dressing? Catalina will work just fine.

6 boneless, skinless chicken
    breasts
18-oz. jar apricot preserves

16-oz. bottle Russian salad
    dressing
1-oz. pkg. onion soup mix

Arrange chicken in a lightly greased 13"x9" baking pan; set aside. Combine preserves, dressing and soup mix in a medium bowl; pour over chicken. Cover with aluminum foil; bake at 350 degrees for one hour, spooning sauce over chicken once or twice during baking. Serves 6.

Keep salad greens fresh longer. Simply wash & dry as soon as they're brought home, wrap in a paper towel and seal in a plastic zipping bag. The towel will absorb any moisture and greens will stay crisp.

Mexicali Casserole

Kellie Duncan
Little Rock, AR

Sprinkle with crushed nacho tortilla chips for a crunchy topping.

1 lb. ground beef, browned
   and drained
6.8-oz. pkg. beef-flavored
   vermicelli mix, cooked
10-oz. can tomatoes with chiles

10-3/4 oz. can cream of
   mushroom soup
1/2 c. milk
8-oz. pkg. shredded Cheddar
   cheese

Combine all ingredients except cheese in a medium saucepan;
mix well. Simmer until heated through, about 5 minutes. Pour into
a lightly greased 3-quart casserole dish; top with cheese. Bake at
350 degrees for 10 to 15 minutes, until cheese melts.
Serves 4 to 6.

Keep a cherished cookbook clean as brand new...
slip it into an oversized plastic zipping bag
before beginning a favorite recipe.

Sheila's Chicken Enchiladas

Sheila Murray
Lancaster, CA

This is very easy and it tastes great. Sometimes I like to garnish it with sliced olives.

2 10-3/4 oz. cans cream of mushroom soup
12-oz. can evaporated milk
10-1/2 oz. can enchilada sauce
13-1/2 oz. pkg. tortilla chips, divided

4 to 6 boneless, skinless chicken breasts, cooked, diced and divided
8-oz. pkg. shredded Cheddar cheese, divided

Mix together soup, milk and sauce; set aside. Arrange half the chips in an ungreased 13"x9" baking pan. Top with half each of chicken, cheese and soup mixture. Repeat layers. Bake at 350 degrees for 30 to 40 minutes, until bubbly. Serves 6 to 8.

Wash greasy dishes and pans in a snap...just add a tablespoon of white vinegar to the hot soapy dishwater. The vinegar will cut right through the grease.

Savory Chicken Romano

Krysta Bickley
Alliance, OH

Can't find chicken cutlets? Place boneless chicken breasts between 2 pieces of wax paper...flatten with a meat tenderizer.

3 T. seasoned dry bread crumbs
3 T. grated Romano cheese
4 thin boneless chicken breast
    cutlets
1 T. olive oil, divided
14-1/2 oz. can diced tomatoes,
    drained and 1/3 c. juice
    reserved

3 cloves garlic, minced
2 T. Kalamata olives, pitted
    and chopped
1 t. balsamic vinegar
1/8 t. red pepper flakes
3 T. fresh basil, chopped

Combine crumbs and cheese in a shallow dish. Coat chicken in crumb mixture on both sides; set aside. Heat 1-1/2 teaspoons oil in a large non-stick skillet over medium heat. Add half the chicken; cook for about 6 to 8 minutes per side, or until juices run clear. Transfer chicken to a plate; keep warm. Repeat with remaining oil and chicken; remove to plate. Add tomatoes, reserved juice, garlic, olives, vinegar and red pepper flakes to skillet. Cook for 2 minutes, stirring occasionally, until slightly thickened. Remove from heat; stir in basil. Spoon sauce over chicken and serve. Makes 4 servings.

For a special dessert, soften 2 pints ice cream
and spread in a graham cracker crust, then freeze.
Garnish with whipped topping and cookie crumbs
or fresh berries. Yummy!

Chicken & Broccoli Alfredo

Beth Cavanaugh
Gooseberry Patch

Hearty and satisfying.

2 T. butter
4 boneless, skinless chicken
   breasts, cubed
10-3/4 oz. can cream of
   mushroom soup
1/2 c. milk
1/4 t. pepper

12-oz. pkg. linguine pasta,
   cooked
10-oz. pkg. frozen broccoli,
   cooked
3/4 c. grated Parmesan cheese,
   divided

Heat butter in a large skillet over medium heat. Add chicken and cook until golden, stirring often. Add soup, milk, pepper, cooked linguine, broccoli and 1/2 cup Parmesan cheese. Heat through, stirring occasionally. Sprinkle with remaining Parmesan cheese. Serves 4.

It's a snap to slice uncooked meat...
pop it in the freezer for 10 to 15 minutes first.

Jen's Micro Chicken Casserole

Jennifer McIntosh
New Bern, NC

A very flexible one-dish dinner that's ready in just a few minutes. Sometimes I'll use leftover roast turkey…leftover or instant mashed potatoes work just fine too.

3 to 4 boneless, skinless chicken breasts, cooked and cubed
14-1/2 oz. can green beans, drained
10-3/4 oz. can cream of mushroom soup
1/4 c. milk
1 c. shredded Cheddar cheese
4 c. mashed potatoes
3-oz. can French fried onions

Mix together chicken, green beans, soup, milk and cheese; pour into a lightly greased microwave-safe 3-quart casserole dish. Microwave on high setting for 5 minutes, or until heated through. Top with mashed potatoes and French fried onions. Heat on high setting for an additional 5 minutes, or until onions are golden. Serves 6.

To freshen a microwave oven, pour a tablespoon of lemon juice into a mug of water. Heat on high setting until boiling and let stand for a few minutes with the door closed, then just wipe clean…no scrubbing.

Chicken Chow Mein

Linda Davidson
Lexington, KY

Most of the ingredients are right in your cupboard.

6-oz. can chicken, drained
4-oz. can sliced mushrooms, drained
10-3/4 oz. can cream of celery soup

5-oz. can evaporated milk
5-oz. can chow mein noodles
1 c. celery, chopped
1 c. cashews, chopped
Optional: cooked rice

Mix together all ingredients except rice. Bake at 350 degrees in a lightly greased 3 to 4-quart casserole dish until golden, bubbly and celery is tender, about 25 to 30 minutes. Serve over cooked rice, if desired. Serves 3 to 4.

For a pantry that's always neat as a pin, place self-adhesive vinyl shelf liner on the shelves... drips and spills wipe clean easily.

Hearty Red Beans & Rice

Kerry Mayer
Dunham Springs, LA

A big bowl of this down-home favorite really hits the spot.

1 green pepper, chopped
1 onion, chopped
1/2 c. green onion, chopped
1/2 c. celery, chopped
2 T. fresh parsley, chopped
3 slices bacon, crisply cooked, crumbled and drippings reserved
1/2 lb. Polish sausage, sliced

2 15-oz. cans kidney beans, drained and rinsed
6-oz. can tomato paste
2-oz. jar chopped pimentos, drained
2 T. catsup
1-1/2 t. Worcestershire sauce
1 t. chili powder
3 c. cooked rice

In a skillet over medium heat, sauté green pepper, onions, celery and parsley in reserved drippings until tender. Stir in bacon and remaining ingredients except rice. Reduce heat; cover and simmer for 30 minutes. Serve over cooked rice. Serves 4.

If a recipe calls for just a partial can of tomato paste, freeze the rest in ice cube trays, then pop out and store in a freezer bag. Frozen cubes can be dropped into simmering soups or stews for added flavor...easy!

Mediterranean Shrimp & Rice

Vickie

*For extra flavor, use the tomato liquid
in place of some of the water.*

2 T. olive oil
1 onion, chopped
2 cloves garlic, minced
7-oz. pkg. rice pilaf mix,
    uncooked
1-1/2 c. water
12-oz. can tiny shrimp, drained
    and liquid reserved

1/4 t. dried oregano
1/4 t. dried mint
14-1/2 oz. can diced tomatoes,
    drained
2-oz. can chopped black olives,
    drained
1/2 c. grated Parmesan cheese

Heat oil in a large skillet over medium heat. Add onion, garlic and
rice mix, setting aside seasoning packet; cook and stir until rice is
golden. Add seasoning packet, water, reserved shrimp liquid and
herbs. Bring to a boil; reduce heat to low, cover and simmer for
10 to 15 minutes, until rice is tender. Stir in shrimp, tomatoes and
olives; simmer for 8 to 10 minutes, until heated through. Sprinkle
with Parmesan cheese. Makes 4 servings.

Keep a pair of kitchen scissors nearby for chopping
bacon, snipping green onions and opening packages...
you'll wonder what you ever did without them!

Cornbread-Topped Beef Bake

Regina Vining
Warwick, RI

*Use a cast iron skillet...pop it right in the oven
for one-pot convenience.*

1/2 lb. ground beef
1 onion, chopped
3 slices bacon, crisply cooked,
   crumbled and drippings
   reserved
10-3/4 oz. can tomato soup
2/3 c. water
2 16-oz. cans black beans,
   drained and rinsed

1 t. chili powder
1/2 t. garlic powder
Optional: 1/4 t. red pepper
   flakes
1 c. shredded Cheddar cheese
8-1/2 oz. pkg. cornbread mix

In a skillet over medium heat, brown ground beef and onion
in reserved drippings; drain. Stir in soup, water, crumbled bacon,
beans and seasonings. Simmer over low heat for 20 minutes,
stirring often and adding a little more water if necessary. Sprinkle
cheese over beef mixture; mix well. Pour into a lightly greased
13"x9" baking pan; set aside. Prepare cornbread batter according
to package directions; spread over beef mixture. Bake at
400 degrees for 20 to 30 minutes, until cornbread is golden.
Serves 6.

Add a delightful crunch to tossed salads with a
sprinkle of sunflower kernels or sliced almonds.

Bean & Chile Burgers

Angela Murphy
Tempe, AZ

*Delicious meatless patties...serve on multi-grain buns
for extra goodness.*

16-oz. can black beans,
   drained and rinsed
11-oz. can corn, drained
4-oz. can green chiles
1 c. cooked rice
1/2 c. cornmeal

1 t. onion powder
1/4 t. garlic powder
salt to taste
2 T. oil
4 sandwich buns, split
Optional: salsa

Mash beans in a large bowl; add corn, chiles, rice, cornmeal, onion powder and garlic powder. Form mixture into 4 large patties; sprinkle with salt. Heat oil over medium heat; add patties and cook until golden on both sides. Serve on buns, topped with salsa, if desired. Makes 4 servings.

Serve burgers on split and toasted English muffins...
a nice change from hamburger buns.

Hungarian Pork Skillet

Robin Hill
Rochester, NY

Serve over spinach fettuccine for added color.

1/4 c. plus 2 T. butter
3 lbs. pork tenderloin, sliced
3 onions, thinly sliced
14-1/2 oz. can diced
   tomatoes
1/2 c. red wine or beef broth

3 T. paprika
3 T. caraway seed
1 c. sour cream
12-oz. pkg. fettuccine pasta,
   cooked

Melt butter in a large skillet over medium heat. Add pork; cook until tender and golden. Remove from skillet; cover and set aside. Add onions; cook and stir until golden, 10 to 15 minutes. Add tomatoes, wine or broth, paprika and caraway seed. Cover and simmer for 30 minutes. Return pork to skillet; stir in sour cream. Heat through over very low heat, about 5 minutes. Serve pork and sauce over cooked fettuccine. Serves 8.

Homemade pizza is terrific for quick dinners.
Simply top an oven-ready crust with sauce, leftover
sliced meats and veggies. Sprinkle with cheese and
pop it into a hot oven until the cheese melts. Yum!

Take-It-Easy Meals

Lots of flavor without much cooking

Lots of flavor without much cooking

★ With a little slicing and dicing, dinner is ready before you know it...scrumptious supper salads, hearty sandwiches and pasta dishes.

★ The supermarket deli is oh-so-handy for flavorful ready-to-eat turkey, ham, chicken and beef...cheese too. Order it sliced as thin as you like or have it sliced thick so you can cube or dice it.

★ For hearty salads in a snap, keep unopened cans and jars of diced tomatoes, black olives, marinated artichokes and chickpeas in the fridge. They'll be chilled and ready to toss with fresh greens or cooked pasta at a moment's notice.

★ Stock up on a variety of flavorful salad dressings and zingy condiments...they can give salads and sandwiches extra zip with no extra effort.

★ Sandwiches don't have to be made with ordinary bread...be creative! Try pita rounds and soft tortilla wraps for a tasty change.

Fresh Tomato & Basil Linguine

Vickie

If ripe garden tomatoes are out of season, roma or cherry tomatoes are good substitutes.

1-1/2 lbs. tomatoes, finely chopped
3 cloves garlic, minced
1 red pepper, chopped
1 bunch fresh basil, torn
1/2 c. olive oil

1 t. salt
pepper to taste
16-oz. pkg. linguine pasta, cooked
Garnish: grated Parmesan cheese

Stir together tomatoes, garlic, red pepper and basil in a large bowl; drizzle with oil. Sprinkle with salt and pepper; mix well and toss with hot cooked linguine. Sprinkle with Parmesan cheese as desired. Serves 6 to 8.

If pasta is on the menu tonight, put a big pot of water on to boil as soon as you arrive home. It'll be boiling in no time.

Fettuccine & No-Cook Tomato Sauce

Audrey Lett
Newark, DE

Delicious...so fresh tasting.

1-1/2 lbs. tomatoes, chopped
4 cloves garlic, minced
16-oz. pkg. fettuccine pasta,
　uncooked
1/4 c. olive oil

8 black olives, chopped
8 green olives, chopped
3 T. fresh parsley, chopped
salt and pepper to taste
Optional: 2 T. capers

Toss together tomatoes and garlic; place in a colander to drain and set aside. Cook fettuccine according to package directions; drain and return to cooking pot. Add tomato mixture and remaining ingredients. Toss well and let stand for 3 to 5 minutes before serving. Serves 4.

A flexible plastic cutting mat makes speedy work of slicing & dicing...after chopping, just fold it half and pour ingredients into the mixing bowl.

Creamy Garlic & Herb Penne

Stephanie Mayer
Portsmouth, VA

A simple salad tossed with oil & vinegar dressing goes well with this lightly sauced pasta.

5-oz. pkg. garlic & herb cheese
   spread, softened
1/4 c. grated Parmesan cheese
1/2 lb. tomatoes, coarsely
   chopped

salt and pepper to taste
12-oz. pkg. penne pasta,
   uncooked
1/4 c. fresh chives, chopped
1/4 c. fresh parsley, chopped

Combine cheese spread, Parmesan cheese, tomatoes, salt and pepper in a large bowl; set aside to warm to room temperature. Cook pasta according to package directions; drain, reserving 1/4 cup hot pasta water. Immediately add pasta to cheese mixture; sprinkle with herbs. Stir gently, adding one to 2 tablespoons reserved water to desired consistency. Serves 4.

Add some fresh broccoli or asparagus to a favorite pasta recipe...simply drop chopped veggies into the pasta pot about halfway through the cooking time. Pasta and veggies will be tender at about the same time.

Texas Steak Sandwiches

Julie Horn
Chrisney, IN

My husband and I love these hearty sandwiches. They're super simple to make...when guests drop by, I can whip them up in no time, and everyone begs for the recipe.

8 slices frozen Texas toast
1-1/2 lbs. deli roast beef, sliced
steak sauce to taste

8 slices provolone cheese
Optional: sliced green pepper
    and red onion, sautéed

Bake Texas toast at 425 degrees for about 5 minutes per side, until softened and lightly golden; set aside. Warm roast beef in a skillet over medium heat until most of juices have evaporated; stir in steak sauce. Divide beef evenly among 4 toast slices; top with cheese slices, pepper and onion, if desired. Place beef-topped toast and remaining toast on a baking sheet; bake at 425 degrees until cheese is melted. Combine to form sandwiches.
Makes 4 sandwiches.

If family members will be dining at different times, fix sandwiches ahead of time, wrap in aluminum foil and refrigerate. Pop them into a toaster oven or under a broiler to heat...fresh, tasty and ready when you are!

Take-It-Easy Meals

Creole Steak Rolls

Claire Bertram
Lexington, KY

Zesty and satisfying!

1/3 c. mayonnaise
2 T. Creole mustard
2 to 3 drops hot pepper sauce
4 frozen country-fried beef
    steak patties

4 onion rolls, split
4 slices Muenster cheese
Garnish: lettuce leaves, sliced
    tomato, sliced red onion

Blend together mayonnaise, mustard and sauce in a small bowl and set aside. Place steak patties on a microwave-safe dish; microwave according to package directions. Spread rolls with mayonnaise mixture. Place one patty on the bottom of each roll; top with cheese, lettuce, tomato and onion. Add tops of rolls and serve immediately. Makes 4 sandwiches.

Serve up tasty squash fries instead of the same ol' French fries. Peel a butternut squash, slice into fries and place on a lightly greased baking sheet. Bake at 425 degrees for about 40 minutes, turning once, until tender. Salt to taste. Yum!

Grilled Cuban Sandwiches

Beth Kramer
Port Saint Lucie, FL

A Caribbean favorite...yummy!

4 submarine rolls, split
4 t. mustard
1/3 lb. roast pork, thinly sliced
4 slices Swiss cheese

1/3 lb. deli baked ham, thinly
  sliced
dill pickle slices
1 T. butter, softened

Spread rolls with mustard; layer bottoms of rolls with pork, cheese, ham and pickles. Add tops of rolls; lightly spread outside surface of rolls with butter. Grill on a hot griddle over medium heat until lightly toasted and cheese is melted. Makes 4 sandwiches.

For a quick & tasty side, slice fresh tomatoes in half and sprinkle with minced garlic, Italian seasoning and grated Parmesan cheese. Broil until tomatoes are tender, about 5 minutes...scrumptious!

Roast Beef & Pepper Panini

Jennie Gist
Gooseberry Patch

Your favorite sandwich shop couldn't make them any tastier.

8 thick slices Italian bread
8 slices deli roast beef
4 slices mozzarella cheese
8-oz. jar roasted red peppers,
    drained and chopped

2 T. green olives with
    pimentos, diced
1 T. olive oil

Top 4 slices bread with roast beef, cheese, peppers and olives; add remaining bread slices. Brush oil lightly over both sides of sandwiches. Heat a large skillet over medium heat; add sandwiches and cook for 2 to 3 minutes on each side until golden and cheese has melted. Slice sandwiches in half to serve. Makes 4 sandwiches.

Let your countertop meat grill do double duty...
it's great for grilling thick sandwiches to perfection.

Dressed-Up Dogs

Shawna Weathers
Judsonia, AR

My mother used to fix hot dogs this way when I was a child,
and now my own children are happy when I do too.

8 hot dogs
8 slices rye bread
mayonnaise-type salad
   dressing to taste

Optional: mustard to taste
2 kosher dill pickles, sliced
   lengthwise
4 slices Swiss cheese

Slice hot dogs lengthwise, taking care not to cut all the way
through. Arrange hot dogs cut-side down on a hot griddle sprayed
with non-stick vegetable spray. Cook on each side until golden
and warmed through; set aside. Spread 4 slices bread with salad
dressing and mustard, if using; top each with 2 pickle slices,
2 hot dogs and one slice cheese. Top with remaining 4 slices
bread. Makes 4 sandwiches.

If busy kids can't get home for dinner, take it
to them. Pack a tailgating basket and enjoy
picnicking with them at the ballpark. Be sure
to pack extra for hungry team members.

Corned Beef Cheeseburgers

Sharon Crider
Junction City, KS

A tasty change from the usual burgers.

12-oz. can corned beef, chopped
1/4 c. onion, diced
3 T. mayonnaise
1 T. mustard
1-1/2 t. horseradish

8 hamburger buns, split
  and toasted
8 slices American cheese
3 T. butter

Combine corned beef, onion, mayonnaise, mustard and horseradish in a bowl; mix well. Spread corned beef mixture on toasted bottom halves of buns. Top with cheese slices. Broil until cheese melts; spread butter evenly among toasted bun tops. Place toasted bun tops over corned beef mixture. Makes 8 sandwiches.

Turn leftover bits & pieces of cheese from the fridge into a scrumptious sandwich topping. Just shred cheese and stir in enough mayo to make a spreading consistency. Serve on crusty bread...yum!

No-Bake Ham Pizza

Zoe Bennett
Columbia, SC

*Sprinkle on some diced carrot and chopped broccoli too...
the kids will love eating their veggies.*

1/2 c. cream cheese with
   chives, softened
1/4 c. mayonnaise
2 T. horseradish sauce
1 Italian pizza crust
1-1/2 c. cooked ham, chopped

1-1/2 c. roma tomatoes,
   chopped
1/2 c. lettuce, shredded
1/4 c. creamy Italian salad
   dressing

Combine cream cheese, mayonnaise and horseradish sauce in a
small bowl; blend well. Spread over pizza crust. Top with ham,
tomatoes and lettuce; drizzle with salad dressing. Cut into wedges
and serve immediately. Serves 6.

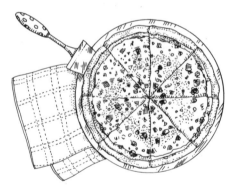

Have an all-finger-food dinner. Slice No-Bake Ham
Pizza into small squares...serve with BBQ cocktail weenies
and fresh carrot and celery dippers with cups of creamy
salad dressing. What fun!

Dilly Egg Salad Sandwiches

Dana Cunningham
Lafayette, LA

A new twist on an old standby.

8 eggs, hard-boiled, peeled
   and chopped
1/4 c. mayonnaise
1-1/2 T. Dijon mustard
1/4 c. celery, minced
2 T. green onion, minced

2 T. fresh dill, chopped
2 t. white vinegar
salt and pepper to taste
8 slices country-style bread
2 c. shredded lettuce

Combine all ingredients except lettuce and bread; mix well and chill until serving time. Divide egg salad evenly among 4 slices of bread; top with lettuce and remaining bread slices. Serve immediately. Makes 4 sandwiches.

Chop up hard-boiled eggs for egg salad quickly...
just use a pastry blender.

Hula Ham Wraps

Nancy Wise
Little Rock, AR

Use green or red flour tortillas for a twist.

3/4 lb. deli ham, sliced into
   strips
20-oz. can pineapple tidbits,
   drained
2 carrots, peeled and shredded
1 head Napa cabbage, shredded

1 c. sour cream
1/4 c. white wine vinegar
1 t. salt
1/4 t. pepper
Optional: 1 t. caraway seed
12 10-inch flour tortillas

Combine ham, pineapple, carrots and cabbage in a large bowl; set aside. In a separate bowl, whisk together sour cream, vinegar, salt, pepper and caraway seed, if using. Pour over ham mixture; toss. Divide among tortillas and roll into wraps. Serves 6.

Even a simple sandwich supper with family can be memorable when it's thoughtfully served. Use the good china, set out cloth napkins and a vase of fresh flowers... after all, who's more special than your family?

Take-It-Easy Meals

Chicken & Veggie Wraps

Jackie Smulski
Lyons, IL

Pick up a package of grilled chicken strips at the supermarket to use...wraps will be ready to eat in a flash.

8-oz. container garden vegetable
   cream cheese, softened
3 T. mayonnaise
4 8-inch flour tortillas
2 c. romaine lettuce, shredded

1/4 c. sun-dried tomatoes,
   thinly sliced
8 slices provolone cheese
4 green onions, sliced
2 c. cooked chicken, diced

Whisk together cream cheese and mayonnaise until well blended; spread over tortillas. Top with lettuce, tomatoes, cheese, onions and chicken. Roll up tightly; cut in half to serve. Serves 4.

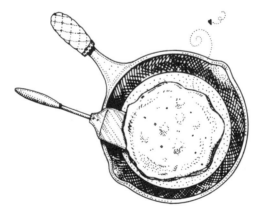

Flour tortillas are tastiest when warmed. Stack tortillas between moistened paper towels and microwave on high setting for 20 to 30 seconds...easy!

Mediterranean Turkey Pitas

Tina Wright
Atlanta, GA

*Try marinated olive salad instead of
the veggies for a different taste.*

2 T. mayonnaise
2 whole-wheat pita rounds,
   halved
1/4 c. smoked deli turkey,

sliced
1 c. marinated vegetable salad,
   drained and chopped
1/2 c. crumbled feta cheese

Spread mayonnaise inside pitas. Fill with turkey, vegetables and
cheese. Serves 2.

Crabby Avocado Salad

Suzanna Simpson
Rohrersville, MD

*For delicious wrap sandwiches, arrange sliced avocados on soft
flour tortillas, top with crabmeat mixture and roll up.*

1 lb. crabmeat
3 T. mayonnaise
1 t. dry mustard

1/2 c. celery, chopped
salt and pepper to taste
2 avocados, pitted and halved

Combine crabmeat, mayonnaise, mustard, celery, salt and pepper;
mix well. Top each avocado half with a scoop of crabmeat
mixture. Makes 4 servings.

A healthy light wrap for smaller appetites...place sandwich
toppings on lettuce leaves instead of bread and roll up.

Cool Gazpacho Soup

Sharon Tillman
Hampton, VA

So refreshing on a steamy day. Garnish with thin slices of lemon.

3 tomatoes, chopped
2 cucumbers, peeled and
   chopped
1/2 red onion, chopped
1 green pepper, chopped
1 yellow pepper, chopped

1 clove garlic, minced
32-oz. bottle cocktail
   vegetable juice
1 T. olive oil
1 T. lemon juice

Combine all ingredients in a deep bowl; mix gently. Cover and refrigerate for at least 4 hours; serve chilled. Makes 6 servings.

Take it easy and have a leftovers night once a week.
Set out leftovers so everyone can choose their favorite.
End with ice cream for dessert...what could be simpler?

Kelly's Special Chicken Salad Pitas

Kelly Reece
Oshkosh, NE

This chicken salad is delicious served on bakery-fresh croissants or over quartered ripe tomatoes too.

1 c. cooked chicken, diced
1 Granny Smith apple, cored,
   peeled and diced
1/2 onion, diced
1/4 c. Swiss cheese, diced
1 to 2 stalks celery, chopped

1/2 c. mayonnaise
1/4 c. mayonnaise-type
   salad dressing
1 T. lemon juice
salt and pepper to taste
2 pita rounds, halved

Mix together all ingredients except pita bread. Spoon into pita pockets. Serves 2.

Stir up a pitcher of pink lemonade for dinner.
Combine 3-1/4 cups water, 1/2 cup sugar and
1/2 cup lemon juice. Stir until sugar dissolves and
add a little maraschino cherry juice to tint it pink.
Serve over ice...so refreshing!

Take-It-Easy Meals

The Ultimate Shrimp Sandwich

Karen Pilcher
Burleson, TX

Treat the family to this scrumptious recipe.

3/4 lb. cooked shrimp, chopped
1/4 c. green pepper, chopped
1/4 c. celery, chopped
1/4 c. cucumber, chopped
1/4 c. tomato, diced
1/4 c. green onion, chopped
1/4 c. mayonnaise

Optional: hot pepper sauce
  to taste
6 split-top rolls, split and
  lightly toasted
2 T. butter, softened
1 c. shredded lettuce

Combine shrimp, vegetables and mayonnaise; toss well. Set aside. Spread rolls evenly with butter; divide lettuce among rolls. Top with shrimp mixture. Serves 6.

Thank you for the world so sweet,
Thank you for the food we eat.
Thank you for the birds that sing,
Thank you, God, for everything.

-Edith Rutter-Leatham

Twistin' Chicken Salad

Marlene Darnell
Newport Beach, CA

*Substitute your favorite creamy salad dressing for
the barbecue sauce, if you like.*

16-oz. pkg. rotini pasta,
    cooked and chilled
2 c. grilled chicken, shredded
1 c. corn
1/2 c. canned black beans,
    drained and rinsed
1 red pepper, chopped
1 yellow pepper, chopped

1 red onion, chopped
1/2 c. fresh cilantro, chopped
3/4 c. White Barbecue Sauce
3 T. lime juice
Optional: 1 jalapeño pepper,
    seeded and chopped
1/4 c. water
salt and pepper to taste

Place cooked pasta in a large bowl; stir in remaining ingredients
except water, salt and pepper. Add water, one tablespoon at a
time, until desired consistency is reached. Sprinkle with salt and
pepper. Serve immediately or cover and refrigerate overnight.
Serves 6 to 8.

White Barbecue Sauce:

1 c. mayonnaise
1 c. cider vinegar
1 T. lemon juice

1-1/2 T. pepper
1/2 t. salt
1/4 t. cayenne pepper

Mix all ingredients together; refrigerate for 8 hours or overnight.

For cold pasta salads, rinse cooked pasta under cold
water and drain well...it will be tender and not mushy.

Antipasto Chicken Plate

Lynda Robson
Boston, MA

*Add your favorite veggies, use turkey instead of chicken...
this is a very flexible recipe!*

3 c. romaine lettuce, torn
2 c. cooked chicken, cubed
1 c. deli salami, cubed
1 c. mozzarella cheese, cubed
2 c. cauliflower flowerets

1 cucumber, diced
1 tomato, chopped
1 yellow pepper, chopped
1/2 c. zesty Italian salad
  dressing

Arrange lettuce on a large platter. Top with remaining ingredients; drizzle with salad dressing. Serves 6.

Pick up a roast chicken at the deli for 2 easy meals in one. Serve it hot the first night, then slice or cube the rest to become the delicious start of a salad, soup or sandwich supper the next.

Tuna-Spaghetti Vinaigrette

Connie Hilty
Pearland, TX

A light, fresh-tasting salad that's perfect for a summer evening.

1/3 c. red wine vinegar
2 T. lemon juice
1 clove garlic, minced
1 t. pepper
salt to taste
1 c. olive oil
4 c. roma tomatoes, chopped

4 c. angel hair pasta, cooked
  and cooled
2 4-1/4 oz. cans chopped
  black olives, drained
6-oz. can tuna, drained
1/2 c. fresh basil, chopped

Whisk together first 5 ingredients in a deep bowl. Slowly add oil, whisking continuously, until well blended. Set aside. Combine tomatoes, pasta, olives and vinegar mixture to taste; toss well. Add tuna and basil; toss. Serve immediately. Serves 4.

Stock the cupboard with cans of chicken and tuna.
They make it oh-so easy to toss together all kinds
of quick & tasty meals.

Fajita & Bowties Salad Bowl

Jennifer Eveland-Kupp
Temple, PA

A spicy twist on pasta salad.

1/4 c. lime juice
1 T. ground cumin
1/2 t. chili powder
1/2 c. fresh cilantro, chopped
1/2 c. olive oil
15-oz. can black beans,
    drained and rinsed

11-oz. can corn, drained
1 c. salsa
2 tomatoes, chopped
8-oz. pkg. bowtie pasta, cooked
2 c. tortilla chips, crushed
1 c. shredded Cheddar cheese

Combine lime juice and spices in a food processor or blender. Process until almost smooth; drizzle in oil and process until blended. Set aside. In a large bowl, combine beans, corn, salsa, tomatoes, pasta and lime juice mixture; toss to combine. Gently mix in tortilla chips and cheese. Serves 4.

Cheese graters wash up in a snap...spray with non-stick vegetable spray before grating.

Orange-Wild Rice Chicken Salad

Rhonda Reeder
Ellicott City, MD

An unusual mixture that's scrumptious.

6-oz. pkg. long grain & wild
   rice, prepared
2 c. cooked chicken breast,
   shredded
1 c. sugar snap peas

11-oz. can mandarin oranges,
   drained
1/2 c. honey-Dijon salad
   dressing

Combine all ingredients in a large bowl; mix well. Chill until
serving time. Serves 4.

When draining canned fruit, freeze the juice in ice cube
trays...oh-so handy for adding a little sweetness to
marinades and dressings.

Country Artichoke & Turkey Salad

Geneva Rogers
Gillette, WY

We love this salad with its hearty, chunky ingredients.

2 6-oz. jars marinated
   artichokes, drained and
   marinade reserved
2 T. balsamic vinegar
1/4 t. pepper
4 c. mixed salad greens

8-oz. pkg. mushrooms, halved
1/2 lb. deli turkey, cubed
1 c. mozzarella cheese, cubed
2 tomatoes, cut into wedges
2 T. grated Parmesan cheese

Stir together reserved marinade, vinegar and pepper in a small bowl; set aside. In a large bowl, toss together remaining ingredients; add half of marinade mixture. Toss to coat; serve with remaining marinade mixture. Serves 6.

Mom's Special Salad

Keep chilled dinner salads fresh & tasty...serve in
an old-fashioned stoneware bowl that
will stay cool longer.

Ranchero Chicken & Bean Salad

Geralyn Hurley
McFarland, WI

I like to serve this salad in crunchy tortilla bowls.

3/4 c. ranch salad dressing
2 T. fresh cilantro, chopped
1/2 t. chili powder
1 t. lime juice
15-oz. can black beans, drained and rinsed
11-oz. can sweet corn & diced peppers, drained
1 red pepper, sliced into thin strips
1/3 c. green onion, sliced
6 c. romaine lettuce, torn
1-1/2 c. cooked chicken, sliced into strips

Combine first 4 ingredients in a small bowl; stir well and set aside. In a large salad bowl, toss together beans, corn, pepper and onion. Arrange lettuce on individual serving plates; top with bean mixture and chicken strips. Drizzle with dressing and serve. Serves 2 to 4.

Top Tex-Mex salads with crunchy tortilla strips for a fun change from croutons. Cut corn tortillas into narrow strips and place on a baking sheet. Spritz with non-stick vegetable spray and bake at 400 degrees for 5 to 7 minutes, until crisp.

Spinach, Chicken & Bacon Salad

Laura Fuller
Fort Wayne, IN

Not a spinach fan? Try spring mix or romaine lettuce.

6 c. baby spinach
2 c. cooked chicken, chopped
1/2 c. crumbled feta cheese
6 slices bacon, crisply cooked,
    crumbled and 1 T.
    drippings reserved

1/2 c. favorite creamy salad
    dressing

Combine spinach, chicken, cheese and crumbled bacon in a large
salad bowl; set aside. Whisk reserved warm drippings into salad
dressing; drizzle half over salad. Gently toss to combine; serve
with remaining dressing on the side. Serves 4.

Quickly dry lettuce with a salad spinner. You may
even find the kids think it's fun to help you with it!

Turkey-Shrimp Macaroni Salad

Nan Wysock
New Port Richey, FL

Always popular at potlucks...the condensed milk gives it a sweet, creamy taste that goes well with the fruit.

6 c. elbow macaroni, uncooked
6 c. cooked turkey, cubed
2 c. cooked small shrimp, cleaned
20-oz. can pineapple chunks, drained
16-oz. can sliced peaches, drained and diced
1 c. celery, sliced

1/2 c. green onion, sliced
14-oz. can sweetened condensed milk
1/2 c. lemon juice
1/2 c. oil
1/4 t. Dijon mustard
1/2 t. salt
1/8 t. lemon-pepper seasoning

Cook pasta according to package directions; drain. Combine pasta and next 6 ingredients in a very large bowl. In a separate bowl, blend together condensed milk, lemon juice, oil, mustard, salt and seasoning; mix well. Pour over salad; toss to coat. Cover and chill for at least 2 hours. Serves 10 to 12.

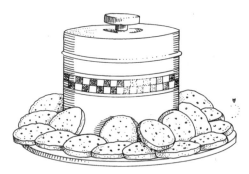

Multi-grain crackers and crunchy bread sticks
can round out salad suppers. Their crispness
makes them perfect with salads and they'll stay fresh
in the pantry much longer than bread.

Slow-Simmered Goodness

Put your slow cooker to work

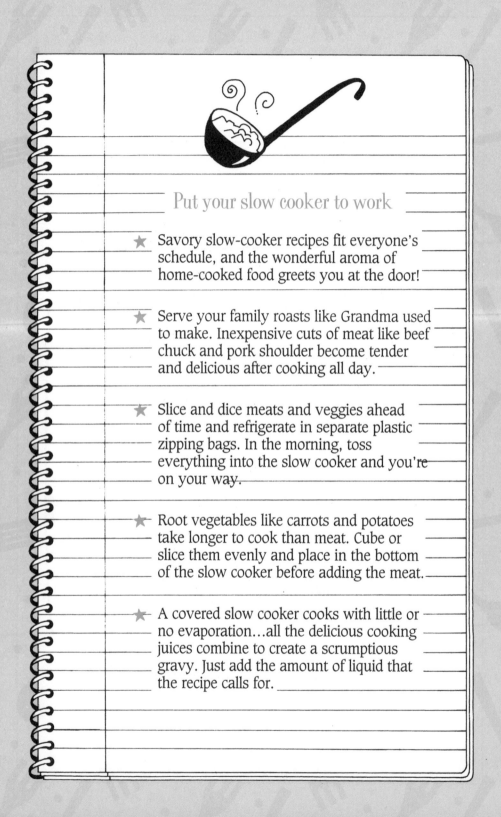

Put your slow cooker to work

★ Savory slow-cooker recipes fit everyone's schedule, and the wonderful aroma of home-cooked food greets you at the door!

★ Serve your family roasts like Grandma used to make. Inexpensive cuts of meat like beef chuck and pork shoulder become tender and delicious after cooking all day.

★ Slice and dice meats and veggies ahead of time and refrigerate in separate plastic zipping bags. In the morning, toss everything into the slow cooker and you're on your way.

★ Root vegetables like carrots and potatoes take longer to cook than meat. Cube or slice them evenly and place in the bottom of the slow cooker before adding the meat.

★ A covered slow cooker cooks with little or no evaporation...all the delicious cooking juices combine to create a scrumptious gravy. Just add the amount of liquid that the recipe calls for.

Slow-Simmered Goodness

Gramma's Smothered Swiss Steak
Jennifer Martineau
Gooseberry Patch

So tender...yummy with mashed potatoes.

1 to 1-1/2 lbs. beef round steak,
   cut into serving-size pieces
1 to 2 T. oil
1 onion, halved and sliced
1 carrot, peeled and shredded

4-oz. can sliced mushrooms,
   drained
10-3/4 oz. can cream of
   mushroom soup
8-oz. can tomato sauce

Brown meat in oil in a skillet over medium heat; drain and set aside. Arrange vegetables in a slow cooker; place meat on top. Mix together soup and tomato sauce; pour over meat and vegetables. Cover and cook on low setting for 8 hours, until meat is tender. Makes 4 to 6 servings.

A large-size slow cooker tends dinner for you all day long. It can easily handle a double batch of a favorite recipe too. Serve half tonight...cool the other half and freeze for a future meal.

Southern Pork Barbecue

Vicki Chavis
Fort Myers, FL

My whole family loves this recipe and my friends ask for it by name. It's a great way to serve a few people or many.

3-lb. boneless pork loin
   roast, trimmed
1 c. water
18-oz. bottle barbecue sauce
2 T. Worcestershire sauce
1 to 2 T. hot pepper sauce

1/4 c. brown sugar, packed
1 t. salt
1 t. pepper
8 hamburger buns, split
Garnish: deli coleslaw

Place roast in a slow cooker; add water. Cover and cook on high setting for 7 hours, or until tender. Shred meat; return to slow cooker. Stir in sauces, sugar, salt and pepper; cover and cook on low setting for one additional hour. Serve on buns, topped with coleslaw. Makes 8 to 10 servings.

For easy slow-cooker clean-up, spray it
with non-stick vegetable spray before filling.
Even easier...use a toss-away plastic liner.

Klein's Green Chile Stew

Linda Neel
Lovington, NM

Great on a cold evening! Use hot, medium or mild green chiles according to your own taste.

1 to 1-1/2 lbs. boneless pork, cubed
2 16-oz. cans pinto beans
2 14-1/2 oz. cans Mexican-style diced tomatoes
2 4-oz. cans diced green chiles
15-1/2 oz. can hominy, drained
1 t. ground cumin
salt and pepper to taste

Place pork in a slow cooker. Top with remaining ingredients; stir. Cover and cook on high setting for 4 to 5 hours. Serves 4.

Uh-oh, you got carried away with the chiles and now dinner is super-spicy! Relief is on the way... just stir in a tablespoon of sugar and a tablespoon of lemon juice to temper the heat.

Brown Sugar Ham

Shelley Turner
Boise, ID

In a word, scrumptious!

2 c. brown sugar, packed
  and divided
6 to 8-lb. bone-in cured
  picnic ham

Optional: 20-oz. can crushed
  pineapple, drained

Spread 1-1/2 cups brown sugar in the bottom of a large slow cooker. Place ham flat-side down in slow cooker, trimming to fit if necessary. Sprinkle remaining brown sugar over ham; top with pineapple, if desired. Cover and cook on low setting for 8 hours. Serves 16 to 24.

Why not get together with friends & neighbors for a potluck dinner? With slow cookers, it's oh-so-easy to prepare a variety of tasty dishes and keep them hot while everyone eats, chats and enjoys visiting.

Cranberry Turkey

Kathy Schroeder
Vermilion, OH

What a simple, easy way to cook turkey...the meat is oh-so juicy and tender. We love it!

1 c. hot water
5-lb. frozen turkey breast
1-1/2 oz. pkg. onion soup mix

16-oz. can jellied or whole-berry cranberry sauce

Pour hot water into a slow cooker. Place turkey skin-side up in slow cooker; set aside. Blend soup mix into cranberry sauce; pour over turkey. Cover and cook on high setting for 2 hours. Reduce to low setting; continue cooking for 5 to 6 hours, or until done. Let stand briefly before slicing. Serves 8.

Take care not to set a hot slow cooker on a cold surface, and don't fill it with cold water to soak after cooking. Sudden changes in temperature can cause the crockery liner to crack or break.

Chicken-Lickin' Pork Chops

Judy Barnes
Hinsdale, NH

Our family's favorite way to eat pork chops...so easy too!

1/2 c. all-purpose flour
1-1/2 t. dry mustard
garlic powder, salt and pepper
   to taste

6 pork chops
1 to 2 T. oil
10-3/4 oz. can chicken &
   rice soup

Combine flour, mustard, garlic powder, salt and pepper; dredge pork chops in mixture. Shake off excess flour and brown chops in oil, about 5 minutes per side. Arrange chops in a slow cooker; pour soup over chops. Cover and cook on low setting for about 6 hours, until tender. Serves 6.

Slow-cook a double batch of beef or pork roast...shred leftovers for scrumptious, quick & easy tacos or burritos.

Sweet-and-Sour Pork

Janice Dorsey
San Antonio, TX

A hearty, filling meal-in-one.

1-1/2 lbs. pork loin, cubed
1 onion, chopped
14-1/2 oz. can chicken broth
10-oz. bottle sweet-and-sour
  sauce
14-oz. can pineapple chunks,
  drained
1 green pepper, cubed
2 c. instant rice, uncooked

Place pork in a slow cooker; top with onion, broth and sauce. Cover and cook on low setting for 8 to 10 hours, or on high setting for 5 hours. Add pineapple, green pepper and rice; mix well. Cover and cook on low setting an additional 20 minutes, until pepper and rice are tender. Serves 4 to 6.

Check the liquid in the slow cooker about 30 minutes before done cooking. If it seems too juicy, just remove the lid and turn the setting up to high...excess liquid will evaporate.

Scrumptious Beef Roast

Joey Curtis
Greeley, CO

*Speed up prep for next time...mix up a double or triple batch
of the tasty seasonings and store in a shaker jar.*

1 onion, sliced
2 potatoes, peeled and cubed
1/2 lb. baby carrots
1 stalk celery, sliced
3-lb. beef chuck roast
12-oz. can beer or
   non-alcoholic beer
1 t. garlic, minced

1 t. garlic salt
1 t. salt
1 t. pepper
1 t. dried basil
1 t. dried oregano
1 t. dried thyme
1/8 t. paprika
1/8 t. nutmeg

Place vegetables in the bottom of a slow cooker. Place roast on
top; pour beer over all. Combine seasonings and sprinkle over
roast. Cover and cook on low setting for 8 hours. Serves 4 to 6.

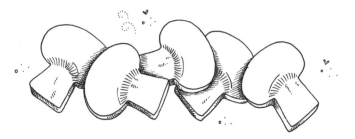

Take advantage of your slow cooker on weekends too.
Put dinner in the crock Saturday morning, then take
the kids on a hike, shop or relax around the house.
Dinner is ready when you are!

Slow-Simmered Goodness

Farmhouse Pot Roast

Cherylann Smith
Elfand, NC

This roast is falling-apart tender and makes its own gravy.

3-lb. beef chuck roast
4-oz. can sliced mushrooms,
    drained
8 redskin potatoes, cubed
1/2 lb. baby carrots

3 stalks celery, chopped
14-1/2 oz. can beef broth
2 c. water
26-oz. can cream of mushroom
    soup

Place roast in a slow cooker; top with vegetables. In a medium bowl, blend together broth, water and soup; pour over roast. Cover and cook on low setting for 6 to 8 hours, until roast is very tender. Makes 6 servings.

"Home" is any 4 walls that enclose the right person.

-Helen Rowland

Irish Corned Beef Dinner

Lisanne Miller
York, ME

Serve with rye bread and spicy mustard for a delicious meal.

3-lb. corned beef brisket
4 to 6 potatoes, quartered
1 lb. carrots, peeled, halved and
    cut into sticks
1 head cabbage, cut into
    wedges

2 onions, quartered
12-oz. can beer or
    non-alcoholic beer
1 bay leaf
2 to 3 c. water

Place corned beef in a slow cooker. Arrange vegetables around meat; add beer, bay leaf and enough water to cover. Cover and cook on high setting for 3-1/2 to 4 hours. Discard bay leaf. To serve, arrange vegetables on a large serving platter. Slice corned beef and arrange on platter. Makes 6 servings.

Potatoes can be peeled and cubed the night before...
just cover them with water before popping
into the fridge. No browning!

Slow-Simmered Goodness

Sausage & Apple Supper

Cathy Hillier
Salt Lake City, UT

Perfect for a cool autumn evening.

14-1/2 oz. can sauerkraut,
    drained, rinsed and divided
1 lb. Kielbasa or other smoked
    sausage, cut into 2-inch
    lengths
3 Granny Smith apples, cored,
    peeled and cut into wedges

1/2 c. brown sugar, packed
3/4 t. salt
1/8 t. pepper
1/2 t. caraway seed
3/4 c. apple juice

Place half of sauerkraut in the bottom of a slow cooker. Top with sausage pieces, apple wedges, brown sugar, salt, pepper and caraway. Add remaining sauerkraut; drizzle apple juice over top. Cover and cook on low setting for 6 to 8 hours. Stir before serving. Serves 4.

It's fine to fill a slow cooker with chilled ingredients, then set the timer to start one to 2 hours later. If yours doesn't have a timer, pick up an automatic timer at the hardware store and plug the crock right into it.

Bayou Chicken

Dawn Dhooghe
Concord, NC

The slow cooker always seems to be going at our house.
This is one of my husband's favorite meals...
and it's so easy to put together!

3 boneless, skinless chicken
   breasts, cubed
14-1/2 oz. can chicken broth
14-1/2 oz. can diced tomatoes
10-3/4 oz. can tomato soup
1/2 lb. smoked sausage, sliced

1/2 c. cooked ham, diced
1 onion, chopped
2 t. Cajun seasoning
hot pepper sauce to taste
3 c. cooked rice

Combine all ingredients except rice in a slow cooker; stir. Cover
and cook on low setting for 8 hours. Serve over hot cooked rice.
Serves 6 to 8.

Grandma's Stew

2 lbs. stew meat   1 cup beef broth
2 onions - chopped
3 carrots - cut up
6 potatoes - peeled - chopped
cook in crockpot 8 hrs.

Adapt family favorites like chili or beef stew to the
slow cooker. A dish that simmers for 2 hours on the
stovetop can generally cook all day on the low
setting without overcooking.

Chicken Italiano

Diane Stout
Zeeland, MI

Full of flavor! Serve over thin spaghetti.

14-1/2 oz. can diced tomatoes,
    drained
7-oz. can sliced mushrooms,
    drained
2-1/2 oz. can sliced black olives,
    drained
1/2 c. onion, chopped
1/2 c. green pepper, diced
3 T. tomato paste

2 T. capers
2 T. olive oil
1 T. garlic, minced
1/2 t. salt
1 t. pepper
1/2 t. dried oregano
Optional: 2 T. red wine
2 lbs. boneless, skinless
    chicken thighs

Combine all ingredients except chicken in a slow cooker; mix well.
Add chicken and stir to coat. Cover and cook on low setting for
8 hours. Serves 4.

Make a fresh-tasting side dish for Chicken Italiano.
Combine 3 to 4 sliced zucchini, 1/2 teaspoon minced
garlic and a tablespoon of chopped fresh basil.
Sauté in a little olive oil until tender.

Beef Chow Mein

*Patsy Roberts
Center, TX*

*Delicious made with pork too...serve over steamed rice
or crunchy chow mein noodles.*

1-1/2 lbs. beef round steak,
    cubed
4-oz. can sliced mushrooms,
    drained
4 stalks celery, sliced
2 onions, sliced
3 cubes beef bouillon

1 c. boiling water
3 T. soy sauce
2 t. Worcestershire sauce
2 T. cornstarch
2 T. cold water
16-oz. can Chinese vegetables,
    drained

Place beef cubes, mushrooms, celery and onions in a slow cooker.
Dissolve bouillon cubes in boiling water; add to slow cooker along
with sauces. Cover and cook on low setting for 8 to 10 hours. One
hour before serving, dissolve cornstarch in cold water; add to slow
cooker along with Chinese vegetables. Serves 4.

Slow-cooked meals mean less time in the kitchen...
more time for family fun! Why not have the kids turn
their favorite drawings into whimsical placemats?
Arrange on a backing of construction paper and
cover with a layer of self-adhesive clear plastic.

Easy Beef Goulash

Pamela Lome
Buffalo Grove, IL

Use sweet Hungarian paprika if you can find it in the spice aisle.

1/2 c. all-purpose flour
1 T. paprika
salt and pepper to taste
1 to 2 lbs. beef chuck steak, cut
   in 1-inch cubes

1 T. olive oil
6-oz. can tomato paste
1-1/2 oz. pkg. onion soup mix
cooked egg noodles

Combine flour, paprika, salt and pepper in a small bowl. Dredge beef cubes in mixture; brown meat in hot oil in a skillet. Place beef in a slow cooker; top with tomato paste and onion soup mix. Add just enough water to cover meat; stir to blend. Cover and cook on low for 5 to 6 hours. Serve over egg noodles. Makes 4 to 6 servings.

Vickie

Some foods like Easy Beef Goulash taste even better the second day. Slow-cook overnight, then in the morning cool and spoon into a food storage container to refrigerate. At dinnertime, reheat on the stovetop until piping hot...mmm!

Down-Home Beans & Ham

Naomi Hoffman
Mansfield, OH

Add a basket of warm buttered corn muffins...yum!

16-oz. pkg. dried lima beans
1/2 lb. ham or bacon, diced
10-3/4 oz. can tomato soup
1 c. water
1 onion, chopped

1 green pepper, chopped
1 t. dry mustard
1 t. salt
1 t. pepper

Cover dried beans with water and let soak overnight; drain.
Combine beans with remaining ingredients in a slow cooker;
mix well. Cover and cook on low setting for 7 to 10 hours,
or on high setting for 4 to 5 hours, adding a little more water
if needed. Serves 4.

Keep a big roll of wide white freezer paper on hand for
casual get-togethers...party tables can be covered in a
snap and the paper can be tossed out afterwards.

Slow-Simmered Goodness

Best-Ever Pork Roast

Sherrill Williams
Fairfield, TN

Good enough for a holiday meal, easy enough for everyday.

4 to 5-lb. boneless pork roast
salt and pepper to taste
1 T. oil
1 clove garlic, slivered
2 onions, sliced
2 bay leaves

1 whole clove
1 c. hot water
2 T. soy sauce
2 T. cornstarch
1/4 c. cold water

Rub roast with salt and pepper. Make several slits in roast with a knife tip; insert garlic. Brown roast in oil in a skillet; set aside. Place one sliced onion in slow cooker; add roast, remaining onion, bay leaves, clove, water and soy sauce. Cover; cook on low setting for 10 to 12 hours, or on high setting for 4 to 5 hours. Remove roast; keep warm. Discard bay leaves and clove. To make gravy, shake together cornstarch and water in a small jar. Add to slow cooker; cover and cook on high setting for 15 to 20 minutes. Serves 8 to 10.

Turn a slow-cooker roast into a complete meal.
Arrange sliced carrots and potatoes in the crock,
then top with the roast...easy and oh-so-tasty!

Country-Style Beef Stew

Jennifer Vallimont
Kersey, PA

For a thicker stew, mix 1/4 cup all-purpose flour and 1/2 cup water, slowly add to stew at end of cooking time and stir constantly until thickened.

2 lbs. stew beef, cubed
1/4 c. all-purpose flour
1/2 t. pepper
2 T. Worcestershire sauce
5 potatoes, peeled and cubed

5 carrots, peeled and diced
1 stalk celery, diced
1/4 c. onion, diced
1-1/2 c. beef broth
1 c. peas

Place stew meat in a slow cooker. Mix flour with pepper and pour over meat; stir to coat. Add remaining ingredients except peas; mix well. Cover and cook on low setting for 10 to 12 hours, or on high setting for 5 to 6 hours. Stir in peas 30 minutes before serving. Serves 4 to 6.

Patience, please! Lifting the lid of the slow cooker will increase the cooking time...try not to peek until food is nearly cooked.

Penn Dutch Chicken Pot Pie

Amy Bachman
Waterville, PA

My stepmother, Rose, gave me this recipe...everyone loves it!
This old-fashioned pot pie is made with noodles
instead of a pie crust topping.

1-1/2 lbs. boneless, skinless
  chicken
6 c. water
1 c. onion, chopped
1 T. chicken bouillon granules
2 c. potatoes, peeled and cubed

3 c. bowtie pasta, uncooked
Optional: 1/2 c. celery, sliced
10-1/2 oz. can chicken gravy
1 t. seasoned salt
1/8 t. pepper

Combine chicken, water, onion and bouillon in a slow cooker.
Cover and cook on low setting for 6 to 8 hours. Pour broth from
slow cooker into a stockpot and set aside. Cut chicken into
bite-size pieces; add to broth along with potatoes, bowties and
celery, if using. Simmer over low heat for 15 to 20 minutes,
stirring occasionally. Stir in gravy, salt and pepper; cook for an
additional 15 to 20 minutes. Serves 4.

Soft veggies like peas and spinach don't need to cook
all day. Stir them into the crock in the last 30 minutes...
they'll keep their fresh color and firm texture.

Savory Sausage Stroganoff

Michelle Bailey
Fort Wayne, IN

Hearty and filling.

1 lb. ground pork sausage, browned and drained
10-3/4 oz. can cream of mushroom soup
14-1/2 oz. can diced tomatoes
1/2 c. milk
1/4 c. all-purpose flour

4-oz. can sliced mushrooms, drained
1 t. garlic, minced
1 t. dried basil
1 c. sour cream
8-oz. pkg. wide egg noodles, cooked

Combine all ingredients except sour cream and noodles in a slow cooker. Cover and cook on high setting for 2 to 3 hours, stirring occasionally. Stir in sour cream near end of cooking time; warm through. Serve over warmed noodles. Makes 4 servings.

Speed up a slow-cooker recipe to suit your
own schedule...2 to 2-1/2 hours on low
equals one hour on high.

Slow-Simmered Goodness

Parmesan Chicken & Rice

Tiffany Wolfe
Cumberland, IA

Serve with steamed, buttered fresh broccoli.

10-3/4 oz. can cream of
   mushroom soup
1-1/2 c. milk
1-1/2 oz. pkg. onion soup mix
1 c. long-cooking rice, uncooked

6 boneless, skinless
   chicken breasts
6 T. butter, sliced
salt and pepper to taste
grated Parmesan cheese to taste

Mix together soup, milk, soup mix and rice in a medium bowl; set aside. Arrange chicken breasts in a lightly greased slow cooker; place one tablespoon butter on top of each chicken breast. Pour soup mixture over chicken; sprinkle with salt, pepper and Parmesan cheese. Cover and cook on low setting for 8 to 10 hours, or on high setting for 4 to 6 hours. Serves 4 to 6.

Mix up a zingy oil & vinegar dressing to drizzle over crisp greens. Whisk together 3 tablespoons olive oil, 2 tablespoons white wine vinegar, 1/2 teaspoon minced garlic, 1/2 teaspoon Dijon mustard and 1/3 cup grated Parmesan cheese. Fresh!

Creamy Cheesy Chicken

Dianne Brenes
Waltham, MA

Makes lots of sauce...delicious spooned over noodles or rice.

3 to 4 lbs. chicken
2 T. butter, melted
salt and pepper to taste
2 T. Italian salad dressing mix
10-3/4 oz. can cream of
   mushroom soup

8-oz. pkg. cream cheese,
   softened
1/2 c. white wine or chicken
   broth
1 T. onion, chopped

Brush chicken with butter; sprinkle with salt and pepper. Arrange chicken in a slow cooker; sprinkle dressing mix over top. Cover and cook on low setting for 6 to 7 hours. About 45 minutes before serving, mix soup, cream cheese, wine or broth and onion in a saucepan over low heat; cook and stir until smooth. Pour over chicken in slow cooker; cover and continue cooking on low setting for an additional 45 minutes. Makes 4 servings.

Cook up a big pot of vegetable soup. Save odds & ends of leftover veggies in a freezer bag. Thaw and place in a slow cooker along with 2 cans broth and 1/2 cup quick-cooking barley. Cook on low for 6 to 8 hours. So satisfying!

Slow-Simmered Goodness

Orange-Glazed Chicken

Anna McMaster
Portland, OR

Sweet and delicious.

6-oz. can frozen orange juice
   concentrate, thawed
1 onion, diced
1 clove garlic, minced
1/2 t. dried rosemary

6 boneless, skinless chicken
   breasts
salt and pepper to taste
1/4 c. cold water
2 T. cornstarch

Combine orange juice, onion, garlic and rosemary in a plastic
zipping bag. Add chicken to bag and toss to coat; place chicken
in a lightly greased slow cooker. Pour remaining juice mixture
over chicken; add salt and pepper to taste. Cover and cook on low
setting for 7 to 9 hours. Remove chicken from slow cooker; cover
and keep warm. Mix together water and cornstarch; stir into juices
in slow cooker. Partially cover slow cooker; cook on high setting
until thick and bubbly, about 15 to 30 minutes. To serve, spoon
sauce over chicken. Serves 6.

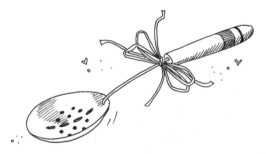

Slow-cooking at a high altitude takes a little longer...
add an extra 30 minutes for each hour of cooking
time called for in the recipe.

Chicken Parmigiana

Diane Tracy
Lake Mary, FL

This is incredibly delicious...so tender you won't need a knife.

1 egg
3/4 c. milk
salt and pepper to taste
2 c. Italian-seasoned dry
   bread crumbs
4 boneless, skinless chicken
   breasts

2 T. oil
26-oz. jar spaghetti sauce,
   divided
1 to 2 c. shredded mozzarella
   cheese
cooked spaghetti

Whisk together egg and milk in a deep bowl. Add salt and pepper;
set aside. Place bread crumbs in a shallow bowl. Dip chicken
breasts into egg mixture; coat with crumb mixture. Heat oil in a
skillet over medium heat; cook chicken just until golden on both
sides. Add one cup sauce to bottom of a slow cooker; top with
chicken. Spoon remaining sauce over chicken. Cover and cook
on low setting for 6 to 8 hours. About 15 minutes before serving,
sprinkle cheese over top; cover until melted. Serve chicken and
sauce over cooked spaghetti. Makes 4 servings.

Frozen veggies are oh-so handy for cooking up tasty
slow-cooker dishes. Thaw them overnight in the fridge
or rinse with cool water before adding...they won't slow
down the heating process.

Slow-Simmered Goodness

Black Bean Chili

Darrell Lawry
Kissimmee, FL

So good any time of year.

1-lb. pork tenderloin
3 15-1/2 oz. cans black beans,
   drained and rinsed
16-oz. jar chunky salsa
1/2 c. chicken broth
1 green pepper, chopped

1 onion, chopped
2 t. chili powder
1 t. ground cumin
1 t. dried oregano
Garnish: sour cream

Place pork in a lightly greased slow cooker; add remaining
ingredients except sour cream. Cover and cook on low setting for
8 hours, or on high setting for 4 hours. Shred pork; return to slow
cooker. Garnish with dollops of sour cream. Serves 4 to 6.

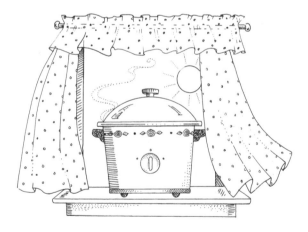

Enjoy hearty, comforting meals all winter long from your
slow cooker...but don't put it away in the summer! Cook up
tender, mouthwatering BBQ sandwiches and other summer
favorites while the kitchen stays cool.

Shrimp & Penne Marinara

Jo Ann

Garnish with extra chopped parsley.

28-oz. can diced tomatoes
2 carrots, peeled and chopped
3 stalks celery, sliced
1 onion, chopped
1 green pepper, chopped
6-oz. can tomato paste
1/2 c. water
1-1/2 t. garlic, minced
2 t. sugar

2 t. Italian seasoning
1/4 t. salt
1/4 t. pepper
1 bay leaf
1 lb. cooked medium shrimp,
 peeled
cooked penne pasta
Garnish: grated Parmesan
 cheese

Combine tomatoes, carrots, celery, onion, green pepper, tomato paste, water, garlic, sugar, Italian seasoning, salt, pepper and bay leaf in a slow cooker. Cover and cook on low setting for 8 to 10 hours, or on high setting for 4 to 5 hours. Increase setting to high; stir in shrimp. Cover and cook for 10 to 15 minutes, until heated through. Remove bay leaf. Toss with cooked pasta; sprinkle with cheese. Serves 6.

Keep frozen shrimp on hand for delicious meals anytime.
Thaw it quickly by placing the shrimp in a colander and
running cold water over it...ready to prepare!

One-Dish Dinners

Fast skillet meals and casseroles

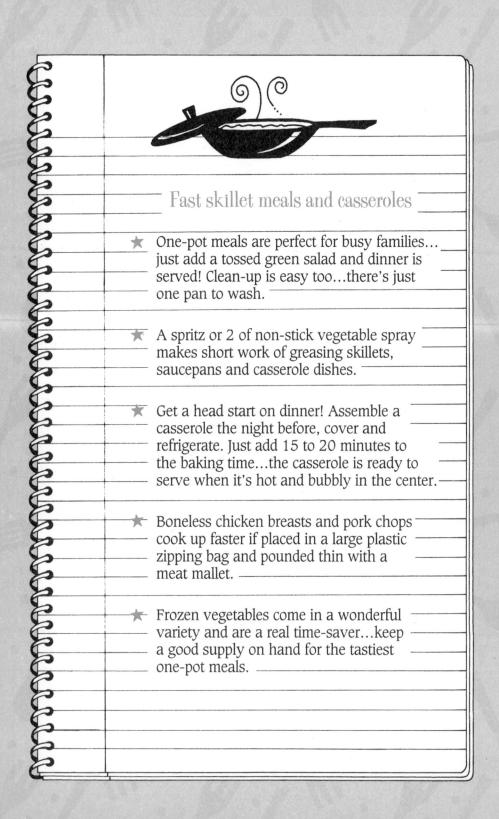

Fast skillet meals and casseroles

★ One-pot meals are perfect for busy families… just add a tossed green salad and dinner is served! Clean-up is easy too…there's just one pan to wash.

★ A spritz or 2 of non-stick vegetable spray makes short work of greasing skillets, saucepans and casserole dishes.

★ Get a head start on dinner! Assemble a casserole the night before, cover and refrigerate. Just add 15 to 20 minutes to the baking time…the casserole is ready to serve when it's hot and bubbly in the center.

★ Boneless chicken breasts and pork chops cook up faster if placed in a large plastic zipping bag and pounded thin with a meat mallet.

★ Frozen vegetables come in a wonderful variety and are a real time-saver…keep a good supply on hand for the tastiest one-pot meals.

One-Dish Dinners

Quick & Easy Beef Stew

Linda Shively
Hopkinsville, KY

Stew simmering on the stove...is there anything better?

1 T. oil
1 lb. boneless beef sirloin
   steak, cut into 1-inch cubes
10-3/4 oz. can French
   onion soup

10-3/4 oz. can tomato soup
1 T. Worcestershire sauce
24-oz. pkg. frozen stew
   vegetables

Heat oil in a large skillet over medium heat; add meat. Cook and stir until browned and juices have evaporated. Add soups, sauce and vegetables; bring to a boil. Reduce heat; cover and cook over low heat for 10 to 15 minutes, until vegetables are tender. Serves 4.

Mmm...freshly baked rolls, so cozy served with stew!
Tie refrigerated bread stick dough into loose
knots and arrange on a baking sheet. Brush with
beaten egg and bake as package directs.

Hamburger Stroganoff

Shannon Kreider
Elizabethtown, PA

My mom always made this for me…it's good comfort food.
It was one of the first meals I made for my husband too.

1 lb. ground beef
1/2 c. onion, chopped
1/4 c. butter
2 T. all-purpose flour
1 t. salt
1/4 t. pepper
1 clove garlic, minced

4-oz. can sliced mushrooms, drained
10-3/4 oz. cream of chicken soup
8-oz. container sour cream
cooked egg noodles

In a skillet over medium heat, brown ground beef and onion in butter. Drain; stir in flour, salt, pepper, garlic and mushrooms. Cook for 5 minutes, stirring constantly. Stir in soup; bring to a boil, stirring constantly. Reduce heat to low and simmer, uncovered, for 10 minutes; stir in sour cream and heat through. Serve over cooked noodles. Serves 4.

A crunchy topping makes any casserole even tastier.
Savory cracker crumbs, crushed tortilla chips or
toasted, buttered bread crumbs are all delicious…just
sprinkle on before baking.

One-Dish Dinners

Enchilada Casserole

Lori Hawkins
Keithville, LA

If you can't find ranch-style beans at your supermarket, just substitute pinto beans and a little chili powder to taste.

1 lb. ground beef, browned
  and drained
10-3/4 oz. can fiesta cheese
  soup
10-3/4 oz. can cream of
  mushroom soup
15-oz. can ranch-style beans

12 6-inch corn tortillas
8-oz. pkg. shredded Cheddar
  cheese
Optional: sour cream,
  diced tomatoes and
  jalapeño peppers

Mix together first 4 ingredients; set aside. Arrange 4 tortillas in a lightly greased 9"x9" baking pan. Spread 4 to 5 heaping tablespoonfuls of meat mixture over tortillas. Repeat layering 2 more times with remaining tortillas and meat mixture; top with cheese. Bake at 350 degrees for 30 minutes, until cheese is bubbly. Garnish with sour cream, tomatoes and jalapeños, if desired. Serves 4.

A tasty side for any south-of-the-border main...stir salsa and shredded cheese into hot cooked rice. Cover and let stand a few minutes, until cheese melts...olé!

Penne & Spring Vegetables

Denise Mainville
Huber Heights, OH

A delicious meatless main or a tasty side for grilled chicken.

16-oz. pkg. penne pasta,
   uncooked
1 lb. asparagus, cut into
   1/2-inch pieces

1/2 lb. sugar snap peas
3 T. olive oil
1/2 c. grated Parmesan cheese
salt and pepper to taste

Cook pasta according to package directions. Add asparagus during the last 4 minutes of cook time; add peas during the last 2 minutes of cook time. Remove pot from heat; drain pasta mixture and return to pot. Toss with olive oil, cheese, salt and pepper; serve warm. Serves 4 to 6.

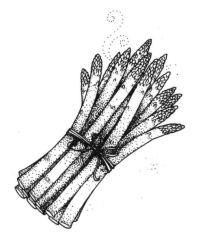

Warmed plates are a nice touch at dinner...just pop them into the oven for about 10 minutes at 250 degrees.

One-Dish Dinners

Apple Orchard Chicken

Christine Schweitzer
York, PA

Sweet and delicious.

4 boneless, skinless chicken
    breasts
1/4 t. seasoned pepper
1 Granny Smith apple, cored,
    peeled and cubed

1 Gala apple, cored, peeled
    and cubed
5 T. crumbled feta cheese
2 T. apple juice

Arrange chicken in a lightly greased 2-quart casserole dish; sprinkle with pepper. Place cubed apples on top of chicken; sprinkle with feta cheese. Drizzle with apple juice. Cover with aluminum foil and bake at 350 degrees for 20 to 30 minutes. Uncover; bake for an additional 10 minutes. Serves 4.

Quesadillas are quick & filling paired with
a bowl of soup or even as a before-dinner snack.
Sprinkle a flour tortilla with shredded cheese, top
with another tortilla and microwave on high until
cheese melts. Cut into wedges and serve with salsa.

Skillet Kielbasa & Veggies

Rosemary Smith
Phelps, KY

This recipe is so simple and convenient. Replace any of the vegetables with others to suit your family's taste.

16-oz. pkg. Kielbasa, sliced
1/4 c. onion, diced
16-oz. pkg. shredded cabbage

15-1/4 oz. can corn, drained
1 lb. yellow squash, sliced

Sauté Kielbasa and onion in a lightly greased skillet over medium heat. Add remaining ingredients and simmer until vegetables are tender, about 8 minutes. Serves 4.

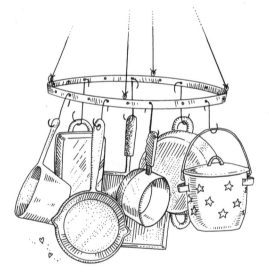

Keep a can of non-stick vegetable spray near the stove... quickly spritz on a casserole dish or skillet for easy clean-up later.

Creamy Spinach Ravioli

Kimberly Pierotti
Milmay, NJ

*Purchase the ravioli and creamed spinach packed in
boil-in bags to make this tasty dish in a snap.*

25-oz. pkg. frozen cheese
  ravioli
2 9-oz. pkgs. frozen creamed
  spinach

grated Parmesan cheese,
  salt and pepper to taste

Prepare ravioli and spinach separately, according to package
directions; drain. Place ravioli in a large serving bowl; top with
creamed spinach, tossing to coat. Add Parmesan cheese, salt and
pepper to taste. Serves 4.

Pick up an extra set of measuring spoons for speedy
meal prep...you'll never need to stop in the middle of
a recipe to wash spoons!

Speedy Meatloaf

Kathy Grashoff
Fort Wayne, IN

We know it's hard to wait...but do allow the full standing time.
The meatloaf will continue to cook for a few minutes after
being removed from the microwave.

1 lb. ground beef
1 egg, beaten
1/2 c. dry bread crumbs
1/4 c. milk

1 T. onion soup mix
2 T. catsup
2 T. soy sauce
1/2 c. shredded Cheddar cheese

Combine all ingredients and shape into a large round loaf. Place in a lightly greased 8" glass pie plate; cover with wax paper. Microwave on high setting for 10 minutes; drain. Cover with aluminum foil; let stand for 10 minutes before slicing. Serves 6.

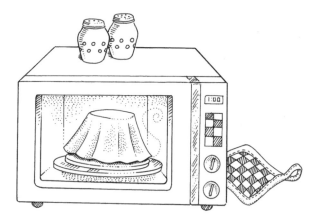

Lay a paper coffee filter over a plate of food before
warming in the microwave...no more splatters!

Saucy BBQ Chicken

Jennifer Rudolph
Ryde, CA

*A yummy recipe for those nights you don't want to
spend a lot of time in the kitchen.*

1-1/2 lbs. boneless, skinless
   chicken breasts
1/4 c. hot or mild salsa
1/4 c. catsup

1 T. onion soup mix
1 T. soy sauce
1/2 t. paprika
1/8 t. cayenne pepper

Arrange chicken in a microwave-safe dish and set aside. Combine
remaining ingredients and spread over chicken to cover, using all
of the mixture. Cover dish with a lid or with microwave-safe
plastic wrap. Microwave on high setting for 25 to 30 minutes.
Serves 3 to 4.

Music sets the tone for pleasant family dinnertimes.
Choose favorites together or listen to something different...
just keep the music low so table talk can continue.

Hearty Potato Soup

Gwen Stutler
Emporia, KS

Serve with grilled cheese sandwiches for a delicious quick meal.

2 T. butter
1 onion, chopped
2 14-1/2 oz. cans chicken broth
6 potatoes, peeled and cubed

2 T. all-purpose flour
2 c. milk
salt and pepper to taste

Melt butter in a large soup pot over medium heat; add onion and cook until tender. Add broth and potatoes; bring to a boil and simmer until potatoes are tender. In a medium bowl, stir flour into milk until completely mixed; add to soup and cook until thickened. Add salt and pepper to taste. Serves 4.

When baking or boiling potatoes, cook a few extras and refrigerate them...you'll be well on the way to dinner another night.

Seafood Bisque in a Snap

Diane Smith
Burlington, NJ

Serve small portions in cups for a delicious party appetizer.

1/4 c. butter
1 onion, chopped
2 stalks celery, chopped
1 T. garlic, chopped
8-oz. pkg. imitation seafood
   pieces
15-oz. can potatoes, drained
   and diced
2 12-oz. cans evaporated milk
1/4 c. water

10-3/4 oz. can cream of
   potato soup
10-3/4 oz. can cream of
   mushroom soup
10-3/4 oz. can cream of
   shrimp soup
10-3/4 oz. can Cheddar
   cheese soup
Optional: 2 T. sherry

Melt butter in a large Dutch oven over medium heat. Add onion, celery and garlic; cook until tender. Reduce heat. Stir in seafood and potatoes; heat through. Add milk, water and soups; stir until smooth and simmer until hot. If using sherry, add just before serving. Makes 4 to 6 servings.

Hollow out round crusty loaves for bread bowls
in a hurry...they make soup even tastier!

Farmhouse Potato Pie

Kelly Alderson
Erie, PA

*A good make-ahead dish for either brunch or dinner.
Assemble, cover and refrigerate, then pop into a
preheated oven before serving time.*

1 lb. bacon, chopped
1 onion, chopped
8 eggs, beaten
1 lb. potatoes, peeled and grated

2-3/4 c. shredded sharp
Cheddar cheese
1/2 t. pepper

Cook bacon and onion in a skillet over medium heat until bacon is crisp and onion is transparent, about 8 minutes. Drain mixture well on paper towels. Combine eggs, potatoes, cheese and pepper in a large bowl; stir in bacon mixture. Spread evenly in a greased 13"x9" baking pan. Bake at 350 degrees for 45 minutes, until set in center; cut into squares to serve. Makes 6 to 8 servings.

The ambition of every good cook...to make something
very good with the fewest possible ingredients.

-Urbain Dubois

One-Dish Dinners

Flash-in-the-Pan Noodle Pizza

Barb Stout
Gooseberry Patch

*You'll have 2 ramen seasoning packets left over...save them
to season vegetables or pasta.*

2 links Italian ground pork
    sausage, casings removed
1 onion, thinly sliced
1 green pepper, thinly sliced
3 3-oz. pkgs. beef-flavored
    ramen noodles, uncooked

1 t. oil
2 eggs, beaten
1 c. spaghetti sauce
1 c. shredded pizza-blend
    cheese
1/4 c. grated Parmesan cheese

In a skillet over medium heat, cook sausage for 2 minutes.
Add onion and pepper; cook until tender and sausage is browned.
Drain; set aside in a bowl. Cook noodles according to package
directions; drain. Stir in contents of one seasoning packet. Brush
skillet with oil; heat over medium heat. Spread noodles evenly
in skillet; pour eggs over top. Cover and cook for one minute,
just until eggs begin to set. Spread with sauce; top with sausage
mixture and cheeses. Cover; cook over medium-low heat until
cheeses melt. Cut into wedges to serve. Makes 6 servings.

Keep fast-cooking ramen noodles on hand for quick meals.
Make a comforting chicken noodle soup by stirring in
shredded chicken and diced veggies or simply top drained
noodles with pasta sauce or gravy. Speedy!

Microwave Sloppy Joes

Coleen Lambert
Casco, WI

A really quick & easy supper...serve with chips and pickle spears in paper-lined burger baskets.

1 lb. ground beef	1/4 c. onion, chopped
1 c. barbecue sauce	4 hamburger buns, split
1/4 c. green pepper, chopped	

Crumble beef into a microwave-safe 1-1/2 quart bowl. Microwave on high for 4 to 5 minutes, until meat loses pink color when stirred. Drain; stir in sauce and vegetables. Cover and microwave on high for 9 to 10 minutes until thickened, stirring once after 5 minutes. Spoon onto buns. Serves 4.

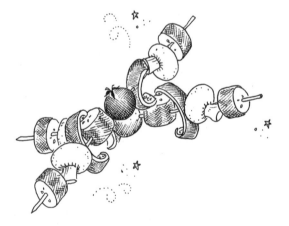

Get kids to eat their vegetables! Serve fresh cut-up veggies with small cups of creamy salad dressing or even peanut butter for dunking.

Spicy Sausage & Rice

Mildred Dearden
Scott City, KS

Turn a boxed mix into a hearty main dish.

1 lb. hot ground pork sausage
1 onion, diced
Optional: 1 green pepper, diced

6.9-oz. pkg. chicken-flavored
   rice vermicelli mix
2-1/2 c. water

Cook sausage over medium heat in a skillet until it begins to brown; add onion and pepper, if using. Continue to cook until sausage is done and onion is tender; drain. Add seasoning packet from rice mix; stir well. Add rest of mix; sauté 3 to 4 minutes, stirring frequently. Add water and bring to a boil. Cover and reduce heat; simmer for 20 to 25 minutes, until rice is tender. Serves 4.

Some skillet meals taste even better the second day!
Why not stir up tomorrow's dinner and refrigerate,
then just reheat before serving, for a time-saver
with a built-in flavor boost.

Amy's Chicken Tetrazzini

Amy Tague
Lebanon, IN

I make this casserole to take to new moms...
they always ask for the recipe!

1/2 c. butter
1/2 c. all-purpose flour
1/2 t. salt
1/4 t. pepper
2 c. chicken broth
2 T. sherry or chicken broth
2 c. milk or whipping cream

8-oz. pkg. spaghetti, cooked
2 c. cooked chicken, cubed
3/4 c. grated Parmesan cheese,
   divided
Optional: 4-oz. can sliced
   mushrooms, drained

Melt butter in a large saucepan over medium heat. Add flour, salt and pepper; cook until bubbly. Add broth, sherry or broth and milk or cream; bring to a boil for one minute. Stir in spaghetti, chicken, 1/4 cup Parmesan cheese and mushrooms, if using; mix well. Spread in a lightly greased 13"x9" baking pan; sprinkle with remaining Parmesan cheese. Bake, uncovered, at 350 degrees for 30 minutes. Makes 6 to 8 servings.

One-Dish Dinners

Potluck Poppy Seed Chicken

Jennifer Langley
Kannapolis, NC

An easy-to-make favorite that tastes great.

4 boneless, skinless chicken
    breasts, cooked and cubed
10-3/4 oz. can cream of
    chicken soup
8-oz. container sour cream

1/2 c. butter, melted
1 sleeve round buttery
    crackers, crushed
2 T. poppy seed

Stir together chicken, soup and sour cream in a lightly greased
8"x8" baking pan. Mix butter, crackers and poppy seed; spread
mixture over chicken. Bake at 350 degrees for 30 minutes, or
until bubbly. Serves 4.

Layer fresh berries with creamy vanilla pudding in
stemmed glasses for a festive dessert, quick as a wink!

Oklahoma Beef Noodle Bake

Mandy Tullous
Duncan, OK

Pure comfort food...perfect for a snowy night.

1 lb. ground beef, browned
  and drained
15-1/4 oz. can corn, drained
10-3/4 oz. can cream of
  chicken soup
10-3/4 oz. can cream of
  mushroom soup

8-oz. container sour cream
1/4 c. pimentos
1/2 t. salt
1/4 t. pepper
3 c. wide egg noodles, cooked
1 c. bread, buttered and torn

Combine all ingredients except noodles and bread in a lightly
greased 13"x9" baking pan. Stir in noodles. Sprinkle bread pieces
evenly over top of casserole. Bake, uncovered, at 350 degrees for
30 minutes. Makes 6 servings.

Make-ahead casseroles are super time-savers for
school potlucks or church carry-ins after work.
Assemble the night before, cover and refrigerate, then
just pop in the oven...soon you're on your way!

One-Dish Dinners

Spicy Salsa Twists

Heather Jacobson
Galesville, WI

Wonderful served with tortilla chips and sour cream.

1 lb. ground beef, browned
    and drained
8-oz. pkg. rotini pasta, cooked
10-3/4 oz. can tomato soup

1 c. salsa
1/2 c. milk
1 c. shredded Cheddar cheese,
    divided

Combine browned beef, rotini, soup, salsa, milk and half the cheese in a large skillet. Cook over medium heat until heated through and cheese is melted; sprinkle with remaining cheese. Serves 5.

Fill the sink with hot soapy water when you start dinner and just toss in pans and utensils as they're used...clean-up will be a breeze.

Creamy Chicken Divan

Lois Bivens
Gooseberry Patch

I got this recipe years ago at a bridge luncheon from a friend of my mother's. It's easy to double...just use a 13"x9" baking pan.

10-oz. pkg. frozen broccoli
   spears, cooked and drained
1 c. cooked chicken breast,
   sliced
10-3/4 oz. can cream of
   chicken soup
1/4 t. curry powder

1/3 c. mayonnaise
1/2 t. lemon juice
1/4 c. shredded sharp Cheddar
   cheese
1/4 c. soft bread crumbs
1 T. butter, melted

Arrange cooked broccoli in a lightly greased 8"x8" baking pan; place sliced chicken over top. Combine soup, curry powder, mayonnaise and lemon juice; pour over chicken. Sprinkle with cheese. Combine bread crumbs and butter; sprinkle over top. Bake at 350 degrees for about 30 minutes, until heated through. Serves 4.

Copy tried & true recipes onto file cards and have them laminated at a copying store. Punch a hole in the upper left corner and thread cards onto a key ring...now you can hang them on the fridge and they'll always be handy.

One-Dish Dinners

Jane's Chicken Casserole

Jane Terrill
Cookson, OK

A tasty way to use leftover chicken or turkey.

2 c. cooked chicken, cubed
2 c. frozen shredded
   hashbrowns, thawed
1 c. frozen mixed vegetables,
   thawed

10-3/4 oz. can cream of
   chicken soup
salt and pepper to taste
1-1/2 c. shredded mild
   Cheddar cheese, divided

Mix together all ingredients, reserving 1/2 cup cheese. Pour into a lightly greased 4-quart casserole dish; top with reserved cheese. Bake at 350 degrees for 30 to 35 minutes, until bubbly. Serves 4.

Microwave baked apples are an oh-so-easy side dish. Core apples nearly through and add a teaspoon each of butter and brown sugar. Place in a microwave-safe dish, cover with plastic wrap and microwave on high for 3 to 6 minutes, until tender. Yum!

One-Dish Cornbread Meal

Patti Davis
Kiowa, OK

Bake this dish in a cast iron skillet like I do...
just preheat it and brush with shortening first.

8-1/2 oz. pkg. cornbread mix
2 eggs, beaten
14-3/4 oz. can creamed corn
1/2 c. milk

4-oz. can chopped green chiles
1 lb. ground beef, browned
    and drained
1 c. shredded Cheddar cheese

Mix together cornbread mix, eggs, corn, milk and chiles; add ground beef and cheese. Pour into a 11"x7" baking pan sprayed with non-stick vegetable spray. Bake at 375 degrees for 40 minutes, or until golden. Serves 4 to 6.

Grandma's good old cast iron skillet is wonderful
for cooking up one-dish dinners. If the skillet hasn't
been used in awhile, season it first...rub it all over
with oil, bake at 300 degrees for an hour and
let it cool completely in the oven.

One-Dish Dinners

Irish Potato-Leek Skillet

Vanessa McClure
Fremont, NE

Leeks are flavorful but can be full of sand. Chop, then rinse very well before using.

1 lb. ground beef
1 leek, chopped
1 clove garlic, minced
6 to 8 new potatoes, peeled
   and diced
3 carrots, peeled and diced
1/2 c. beef broth

1 t. dill weed
1/2 t. salt
1/4 t. pepper
1 bay leaf
14-1/2 oz. can diced
   tomatoes, drained

Cook ground beef, leek and garlic in a large skillet over medium heat, stirring frequently, until beef is browned; drain. Stir in remaining ingredients except tomatoes; bring to a boil. Reduce heat; cover and simmer for 12 to 15 minutes, stirring occasionally, until potatoes are tender. Discard bay leaf; stir in tomatoes and heat through. Serves 4.

Oops...a pan on the stove accidentally scorched.
Don't worry, dinner isn't ruined! Scoop the unburnt
portion into a clean pan, lay a slice of bread on top and
finish cooking. The bread absorbs the burnt odor...
just toss it out when done.

Ham & 2-Cheese Strata

Vickie

An easy dinner for 2...pair with a tossed salad and a fruit cup.

3 eggs
1/4 c. plus 2 T. milk
3 slices sourdough bread, halved
pepper to taste
1 c. shredded mozzarella cheese,
   divided

1 c. shredded sharp Cheddar
   cheese, divided
2 green onions, minced
1/3 c. roasted red peppers,
   chopped
2 thin slices cooked ham

Beat together eggs and milk in a shallow dish; add bread and let stand for 5 minutes. Arrange half of bread in a lightly greased 9"x5" loaf pan; add pepper to taste. Layer with half each of the cheeses, onions and red peppers. Arrange ham slices on top; layer with remaining cheeses, onions and peppers. Cover with remaining bread; pour any remaining egg mixture over top. Bake at 350 degrees until golden and cheese bubbles, about 40 to 45 minutes. Let cool slightly before serving. Serves 2.

If weeknights are busy, why not enjoy a
family brunch together on the weekend? Relax with
each other over tea & coffee, a basket of muffins
and savory Ham & 2-Cheese Strata.
You'll be glad you did!

Chicken & Mushroom Stir-Fry

Kendall Hale
Lynn, MA

*Produce counters now offer a variety of tasty mushrooms.
Use a mixture for added flavor.*

1/4 c. oil
4 cloves garlic, minced
2 T. fresh ginger, peeled and
  minced
4 boneless, skinless chicken
  breasts, thinly sliced

12-oz. pkg. sliced mushrooms
1 jalapeño pepper, minced
1 bunch green onions, sliced
1/4 c. soy sauce
cooked rice

Heat oil in a large skillet over medium-high heat. Add garlic and ginger; cook and stir until golden, about 30 seconds. Add chicken, mushrooms and jalapeño to skillet. Cook, stirring constantly, until chicken is cooked through, about 5 minutes. Remove from heat; mix in onions and soy sauce. Serve over cooked rice. Serves 4.

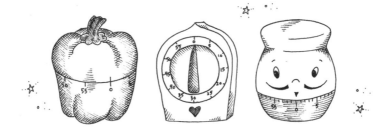

Skillet stir-fries are a versatile way to cook dinner.
Try using sliced pork or beef instead of chicken.
Add any fresh vegetables you have on hand too...tomato,
green pepper and celery are tasty in stir-fries.
Dinner will be on the table in no time.

Index

Index

Index

Send us your favorite recipe!

and the memory that makes it special for you!* If we select your recipe for a brand-new **Gooseberry Patch** cookbook, your name will appear right along with it...and you'll receive a FREE copy of the book.

Share your recipe on our website at
www.gooseberrypatch.com

Or mail to:

Gooseberry Patch • Attn: Cookbook Dept.
2545 Farmers Dr., #380 • Columbus, OH 43235

*Don't forget to include your name, address, phone number and email address so we'll know how to reach you for your FREE book!

Since 1992, we've been publishing country cookbooks for every kitchen and for every meal of the day! Each has hundreds of budget-friendly recipes, using ingredients you already have on hand. Their lay-flat binding makes them easy to use and each is filled with hand-drawn artwork and plenty of personality.

Have a taste for more?

Call us toll-free at
1•800•854•6673

Find us here too!
Join our **Circle of Friends** and discover free recipes & crafts, plus giveaways & more! Visit our website or blog to join and be sure to follow us on Facebook & Twitter!

www.gooseberrypatch.com

Email | Blog | You Tube | f | Twitter | P | Find a Store

U.S. to Metric Recipe Equivalents

Volume Measurements

1/4 teaspoon	1 mL
1/2 teaspoon	2 mL
1 teaspoon	5 mL
1 tablespoon = 3 teaspoons	15 mL
2 tablespoons = 1 fluid ounce	30 mL
1/4 cup	60 mL
1/3 cup	75 mL
1/2 cup = 4 fluid ounces	125 mL
1 cup = 8 fluid ounces	250 mL
2 cups = 1 pint =16 fluid ounces	500 mL
4 cups = 1 quart	1 L

Weights

1 ounce	30 g
4 ounces	120 g
8 ounces	225 g
16 ounces = 1 pound	450 g

Oven Temperatures

300° F	150° C
325° F	160° C
350° F	180° C
375° F	190° C
400° F	200° C
450° F	230° C

Baking Pan Sizes

Square		Loaf	
8x8x2 inches	2 L = 20x20x5 cm	9x5x3 inches	2 L = 23x13x7 cm
9x9x2 inches	2.5 L = 23x23x5 cm	Round	
Rectangular		8x1-1/2 inches	1.2 L = 20x4 cm
13x9x2 inches	3.5 L = 33x23x5 cm	9x1-1/2 inches	1.5 L = 23x4 cm